Passport's Illustrated Guide to
CARIBBEAN
CRUISING
SECOND EDITION

FROM
THOMAS
COOK

PASSPORT BOOKS
NTC/Contemporary Publishing Group

This edition first published in 2000 by
Passport Books
A division of NTC/Contemporary Publishing
Group, Inc.
4255 West Touhy Avenue
Lincolnwood (Chicago), Illinois
60712–1975 U.S.A.

Written by Emma Stanford

Edited, designed, and produced by AA
Publishing.

Library of Congress Catalog Card Number: 98-67242

ISBN 0-8442-1176-1

The contents of this publication are believed correct at the time of
printing. Nevertheless, the publishers cannot accept responsibility for
any errors or omissions, or for changes in the details given in this guide,
or for the consequences of any reliance on the information provided by
the same. Assessments of attractions, hotels, restaurants, and so forth
are based upon the author's own experience and therefore descriptions
given in this guide necessarily contain an element of subjective opinion
that may not reflect the publisher's opinion or dictate a reader's own
experiences on another occasion.
We have tried to ensure accuracy in this guide, but things do
change and we would be grateful if readers would advise us of any
inaccuracies they may encounter.

Published by Passport Books in conjunction with AA Publishing and the
Thomas Cook Group Ltd.

Color separation: BTB Colour Reproduction, Whitchurch, Hampshire,
England.

Printed by: Edicoes ASA, Oporto, Portugal.

Cover photographs: front, copyright © Dave G. Houser; spine © Jan
Butchofsky-Houser/Dave G. Houser Stock Photography.

Contents

About this Book

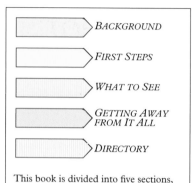

> BACKGROUND
>
> FIRST STEPS
>
> WHAT TO SEE
>
> GETTING AWAY FROM IT ALL
>
> DIRECTORY

This book is divided into five sections, identified by the above color coding.

The best of both worlds – cruising the Caribbean in luxury

Background gives an introduction to the region – its history, geography, politics, and culture.

First Steps offers practical advice on arriving and getting around.

What to See is an alphabetical listing of the places to visit, interspersed with walks and tours.

Getting Away from It All highlights places off the beaten track where it's possible to relax and enjoy peace and quiet.

Directory provides practical information – from shopping and entertainment to children and sports. Special highly illustrated features on specific aspects of the region appear throughout the book.

BACKGROUND

Bahamas
700 Islands

NASSAU
CAY 52
GREAT E UMA
IAMI 112
ELEUTHERA 171
MONTREAL 1,323
ANDRO 103
NEW YORK 1,015
GREAT INAGUA 438
McLEANS TOWN 42
BIMINI 53
SAN SALVADOR 286
BERRY ISLAND 75
GARDEN OF THE GROVES
HYDROFLORA GARDENS

> "The West Indies I behold
> Like the Hesperides of old –
> Trees of life with fruits of gold."
> **JAMES MONTGOMERY**
> *A Voyage Around the World,* 1841

Introduction

Since 1492, when Christopher Columbus set off to sail the ocean blue in search of a western route to the spice islands of the East Indies, travelers have been captivated and enchanted by the Caribbean region. While Columbus signally failed to locate either the Asian mainland, or any spices save pepper, he did discover a chain of alluring sun-drenched islands set in azure seas. Despite all the evidence to the contrary, he called them the West Indies, a name that has stuck, though the term "Caribbean" is more accurate, being derived from the Carib Indians encountered by the early explorers. But one thing is for sure, the West Indies-cum-Caribbean still offers a little bit of heaven on earth to visitors from colder climes.

The majority of Caribbean cruises begin from the world's two busiest cruise ship terminals in Florida (a vacation hotspot in its own right): the Port of Miami and Port Everglades, in Fort Lauderdale. And there can be no doubt that cruising is the ultimate form of travel in the region. Liberated from transportation hassles, lost luggage, and dining dilemmas, cruise passengers can truly relax and enjoy their vacation.

For some, this may extend no farther than a strategically placed chair on the pool deck along with a tall glass of Planter's Punch and a good book. But part of the fun of Caribbean cruising is the variety of destinations visited in a short period of time. Wake up each morning with a new group of islands on the horizon and a different port at the foot of the gangplank – and somebody else has done all the work.

Every island has its own special flavor. Colonial history may be revealed in architecture, as in the toy-town Dutch gables of Curaçao, or there may be distinctive culinary influences, such as the curries of Trinidad and French-Creole dishes of Martinique or Guadeloupe. There's an island to suit all tastes, from super-chic St. Barts to mellow Grenada, from the elegant wafer-thin plantation hotels of Nevis to the eardrum shattering Sunday afternoon reggae sessions atop Shirley Heights in Antigua.

At the end of the day, sightseers and

WHERE WE GO

This guide does not attempt to cover every island in the Caribbean region, or even every corner of the islands listed as more remote spots that are usually inaccessible to cruise passengers with limited time. However, in addition to sections devoted to the main Caribbean cruise embarkation ports of Miami and Fort Lauderdale, you'll find entries covering the top cruise ship ports of call and accessible local attractions on more than thirty Caribbean islands. Bermuda is a summer season favorite anchored out in the Atlantic Ocean, and Key West is a popular mainland stop on several cruise routes.

Glorious technicolor sunsets are a Caribbean specialty

sun-seekers alike can enjoy the sunset fanned by a cooling breeze as the ship gets underway and partake of a gourmet dinner and a spot of entertainment before a turn around the deck beneath the starry skies. Who said the age of romance is dead? It is alive and well – and cruising.

History

1000 BC
First Amerindian tribes, the Ciboney, move to the Caribbean islands from South America.

AD 120
Peaceable fishing and farming Arawak Indians arrive; also from South America.

800
Warlike Carib Indians begin to push the Arawaks from the Lesser Antilles.

1492
October 12: Columbus makes landfall in the Bahamas, at San Salvador.

1493–6
Columbus's second voyage sights Dominica, Guadeloupe, Jamaica, and Puerto Rico.

1498–1500
Columbus's third voyage adds Grenada, Trinidad, and St. Vincent.

1502–4
Columbus's fourth voyage reaches the Central American mainland, via the Cayman Islands.

1503
Juan Bermudez of Spain sights Bermuda.

1513
Juan Ponce de León steps ashore in Florida and names the land after the date of his arrival, La Florida, the Spanish Eastertide Feast of Flowers.

1536
Pedro a Campo of Portugal lands on Barbados.

1565
The Spanish found St. Augustine, Florida.

1600s
The lure of Spanish treasure heralds the "Golden Age" of Caribbean piracy with looting on the high seas. Sugarcane is introduced to the Lesser Antilles; West African slaves are shipped in to work the plantations.

1627
The British settle Barbados.

1648
The French and Dutch divide St. Martin/Sint Maarten.

1655
The British seize Jamaica from Spain.

1671
Denmark colonizes St. Thomas.

1692
The infamous pirate town of Port Royal, Jamaica, is destroyed by an earthquake.

1756–63
The Seven Years' War leads to Franco-British tussles in the West Indies.

1814–15
Europe carves up the West Indies, following the Treaties of Paris at the end of the Napoleonic Wars. Britain grabs the lion's share; the French retain Martinique and Guadeloupe; Cuba, Puerto Rico, and half of Hispaniola go to Spain; and the Dutch and the Danes divide up the remaining smaller islands.

1819
The Spanish relinquish Florida to the U.S.

1834
The Emancipation Act abolishes slavery in Britain and her colonies.

1845
Florida becomes the 27th state in the Union. The First East Indian indentured laborers arrive in Trinidad.

1848–63
The French, then Dutch abolish slavery.

1868
Reconstruction of the southern U.S. results in voting rights for all male citizens of Florida, including African Americans.

1880s
Railroads open up Florida.
1896
Henry Flagler's railroad reaches Miami (and Key West in 1912).
1898
Following the Spanish-American War, Cuba and Puerto Rico are ceded to the U.S.
1902
Mont Pelée erupts in Martinique and destroys the town of St.-Pierre with 30,000 casualties.
1917
The U.S. purchases the Virgin Islands of St. Croix, St. John, and St. Thomas from Denmark for $25 million. Puerto Ricans receive U.S. citizenship.
1920s
The Florida Land Boom creates real estate madness as plots of land exchange hands for fortunes. The market finally collapses with the 1929 Wall Street Crash.
1959
Fidel Castro is elected Prime Minister of Cuba. Mass exodus of refugees starts.
1961
The attempted Bay of Pigs invasion of Cuba by U.S.-backed anticommunist exiles occurs. Jamaica gains independent statehood. Trinidad and Tobago become a presidential republic.
1962
The Cuban Missile Crisis – attempts by the U.S.S.R. to establish rocket bases in Cuba are challenged by President John Kennedy (October 22). The world holds its collective breath until the Russians back down (October 28).
1966
Barbados achieves independence from Britain but remains within the Commonwealth.
1971
Walt Disney World opens in Orlando

with Magic Kingdom, followed by the Epcot Center (1983) and Disney–MGM Studios (1989).
1974
Grenada gains independent statehood.
1978
Dominica becomes an independent republic.
1979
St. Lucia, St. Vincent, and the Grenadines become independent states.
1981
Antigua and Barbuda gain independence.
1983
St. Kitt's and Nevis become independent. A combined U.S. and Eastern Caribbean force makes a "friendly invasion" of Grenada to end the 4-year socialist regime.
1993
Puerto Rico votes against U.S. statehood in favor of continued association with the U.S.
1994
A U.S. "friendly invasion" reinstates Haiti's civilian ex-President Aristide but he is ousted by the voters in 1995. The political situation remains uncertain.
1995
Hurricane Luis causes considerable damage in Sint Maarten/St. Martin and other northeastern Caribbean islands.
1996
Continued activity within Monserrat's Soufrière volcano (erúpted July 1995) causes the southern part of the island and Plymouth to be evacuated.

Nelson in Barbados

Geography

*T*he flat swampy Florida peninsula emerged from the sea 20 to 30 million years ago. Its porous limestone base was formed by massive deposits of sediment packed in deep trenches between extinct underwater volcanoes. The Bermuda archipelago, over 1,000 miles out into the Atlantic Ocean, also has limestone underpinnings, and can claim the world's most northerly coral reefs thanks to the warm waters of the Gulf Stream. To the south and east of Florida, the dozens of islands and tiny cays (small flat islets, pronounced "keys") that make up the Bahama Islands reach down towards the Caribbean region that balances somewhat precariously on the rift of the Atlantic and Caribbean tectonic plates.

The Caribbean Islands – more than 7,000 of them, ranging in size from Cuba (42,800 square miles) to tiny coral atolls just peeking above sea level – begin with Cuba (90 miles off Key West), at the northern extent of the million square-mile Caribbean Sea. Collectively known as the Antilles, they stretch in an arc almost 2,500 miles long and are split into two main groupings: the Greater Antilles (Cuba to Puerto Rico) in the north, and the Lesser Antilles (Virgin Islands to Trinidad) trailing south to the coast of Venezuela. A further distinction is made between the Windward Islands (which receive the brunt of the trade winds off the Atlantic) and the Leeward Islands.

Caribbean scenery varies dramatically from island to island. The mountainous uplands of Jamaica or Puerto Rico could not be a greater contrast to the low-lying limestone and coral Cayman Islands, or the Dutch Leewards, with their Spaghetti Western-style cacti and tortured-looking divi-divi trees. Nowhere is the region's volcanic origins more obvious than in the imposing, jungle-clad volcanic cones of the Windward Islands. Several Windward volcanoes are still alive, and visitors can witness steaming, sulphurous (and smelly) volcanic activity in Dominica, St. Lucia, Guadeloupe, Martinique, and St. Vincent. Conditions also differ between the windward (Atlantic) and leeward (Caribbean) sides of the islands. While the rocky coastline of the former is pounded by Atlantic rollers, the sandy strands of the latter are lapped by gentle wavelets and often further protected by offshore coral reefs.

Soufrière – St. Lucia's "drive-in" volcano in the Windward Islands

The Pitons du Carbet rise above Fort-de-France, Martinique

THE CARIBBEAN

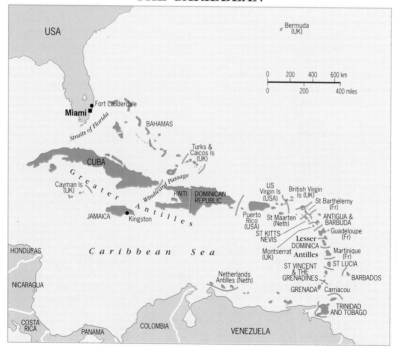

Culture

*L*ike the product óf any great melting pot, Caribbean culture is the sum of its ingredients – and the recipe, in this case, is deliciously exotic. Take a pinch of Spanish influence, a generous measure of French *élan* and British fortitude, add a peck of Dutch and Danish, a dash of Portuguese and American, and then season generously with West African rhythm and Indian spice – *et voila!*

Architecture

A hybrid to the core, Caribbean architecture is both varied and colorful. The islands' colonial masters imported construction techniques from the home country and adapted them to suit the heat. So, for example, you'll find the sturdy stone Georgian buildings of ex-British St. Kitt's and Antigua adorned with louvered shutters and shady balconies. There is a wealth of pretty fretwork decoration, too. Commonly known as "gingerbread," these carved wooden frills and curlicues adorn porches, gables, and eaves all over the West Indies. And they are also popular in Key West, where they were

Spanish-Catholic heritage in Puerto Rico

introduced by the Bahamanian migrants around the turn of the century.

Willemstad's picture-postcard Dutch-gabled waterfront houses on Curaçao are daubed in brilliant pastel shades, a custom that supposedly originated when a 19th-century governor declared that the combination of brilliant sunshine and whitewash was giving him migraines. In other cases, bits of the "old country" were simply transplanted wholesale to the New World, such as the cobbled streets of Puerto Rico's Old San Juan, which are as Spanish as *paella*.

Language

English is the unofficial language of the tourist industry throughout the Caribbean, though it might not help

much in the French islands of Guadeloupe and Martinique. The smaller French territories of St. Barts and St. Martin are more international speaking; while Spanish is the first language of Puerto Rico, but English is widely spoken. The everyday language used by islanders is *patois,* which may seem comprehensible at first (particularly if you speak some French), but then dissolves into gibberish the minute you think you understand. The most common form of *patois* is Creole, a mixture of French and West African laced with occasional English words. If you visit the Dutch Leeward Islands, listen out for *Papiamento,* a truly baffling combination of English, French, Dutch, Spanish, Portuguese, African, and Amerindian elements, developed as a means of communication amongst 17th-century sailors, slave traders, and merchants of all nations.

Choristers wait for morning service to begin in St. Kitts

Music

Music is the heartbeat of the Caribbean. From Trinidadian calypso to Jamaican reggae, you will find that its infectious rhythms are as much a part of the Caribbean experience as palm trees and Planter's Punch. If you get the chance to attend any of the springtime pre-Lenten carnivals or summertime "cropover" festivals celebrating the end of harvest, do not miss out. There are singing and dancing competitions throughout the year, and spontaneous outbursts of both on street corners. Visit the Caribbean at Christmas time and you will be treated to calypso versions of all your favorite carols, too (see pages 132–3).

Religion

Since the earliest European settlers arrived, Christianity has been the official religion of the Caribbean, and many of the oldest surviving buildings are churches. As a rough guide, the former Spanish and French islands are Catholic, and the numerous old churches on British islands are generally Protestant with a high quota of Baptist and Methodist worshippers. Some African animist traditions (basically, the belief that natural objects possess souls) have also survived in Caribbean superstitions, such as the *jumbie* or *duppie* (restless ghost) figures that appear at carnival time. Rastafarianism has spread from Jamaica, where it first appeared in the 1930s as an offshoot of the peaceful black pride movement. Turning away from Western culture, young West Indians looked to their African roots for a new religious and cultural identity. True Rastas are peace-loving, God-fearing types; many are vegetarian teetotalers. Cultural identity is expressed through reggae music, the use of *ganja* (marijuana) to gain spiritual wisdom, and the sporting of rasta (or dread) locks to represent the natural glory of the lion's mane (one title of their former spiritual leader, Emperor Haile Selassie of Ethiopia, was the Conquering Lion of Judaea).

Politics

After more than four centuries of European domination, the Caribbean islands began to shake free of their colonial shackles in the 1950s and 1960s. The majority opted for full independence, but exceptions (though most enjoy varying degrees of self-autonomy) include the Crown Colonies of the British Virgin Islands, Cayman Islands, and Bermuda; the Netherlands' Antilles (though not Aruba, which is autonomous); and the French islands of Martinique and Guadeloupe, which are full-fledged overseas departments of France.

The United States also wields considerable influence in the region with its interests in the U.S. Virgin Islands and Puerto Rico. The U.S.V.I. (St. Thomas, St. Croix, and St. John) are an unincorporated Territory of the U.S. with a self-elected Senate and Governor, and a non-voting delegate to the U.S. House of Representatives. Puerto Rico is a Commonwealth of the U.S., linked to the federal banking system, with an American style government model. While the country enjoys one of the highest standards of living in the region, one issue dominates current Puerto Rican politics: whether the island remains a Commonwealth, or opts for statehood in the 21st century.

This deeply fragmented political scene has done nothing to assist the overall Caribbean economic and social situation. Several attempts at providing the framework for a united front have dissolved into unseemly squabbles, as the various participants seek to preserve their identity and interests. The latest such body, the Caribbean Common Market (Caricom) set up in 1973, has yet to achieve any dramatic steps forward.

However, Caricom has had its eye on the cruise ship industry, which many see as a threat to the all-important tourist trade. The immediate problem of waste dumping at sea by cruise ships has been met with draconian (and fully deserved) fines.

The more invidious problem is the resentment felt by local hoteliers and others in the tourism field who believe their businesses are being undermined and their potential clients lured away by increasingly cheap cruise fares. Caricom's response has been to levy higher taxes on cruise ships, but this does not do much for the bankrupt hotelier, struggling restaurateur, or out-of-work barman.

Pro-American graffiti recalls Grenada's 1983 "friendly invasion" by U.S. troops

FIRST STEPS

"*I remember the black wharves and the slips,*
And the sea-tides tossing free;
And Spanish sailors with bearded lips,
And the beauty and mystery of the ships,
And the magic of the sea."
HENRY WORDSWORTH LONGFELLOW
My Lost Youth, 1807–82

First Steps

A cruising vacation offers, above all else, a trouble-free package that relieves you from the daily hassle of planning and travel, while giving you more time to get out there and enjoy yourself. From the minute you check your luggage on the dockside, you won't have to lug another heavy suitcase until you leave. Life upon the ocean blue is a ball, where daily excursions and evening entertainment are all laid out. All you have to do is simply show up, kick back, and relax. Naturally, your first step is to choose the right cruise, and you will find some helpful hints on pages 178 to 181. But for first-time cruisers, here are a few tips on finding your sea legs.

All aboard!

Embarkation is usually the most gruelling part of any cruise, particularly if you have had a long flight to reach your departure point. Where possible, it is always best to arrange your airport transfers with the cruise line through your travel agent.

When you check in, cruise line staff will check your ticket and identification. Your passport or ID may be taken into safekeeping to be returned at the end of your trip. After a brief photo call for the ship's photographer as you head up the gangway, a steward will escort you to your cabin. Make sure everything is in order. Register any complaints immediately.

Celebrity Cruises' *Zenith*

Life on the ocean wave is a stylish affair for cruise passengers

Who's who?

Your cruise ship will be run by the "crew" under the command of the captain. With the exception of the captain himself, who may appear at official drinks parties and hosts the much sought-after Captain's Table in the dining room, the crew are largely invisible from the passenger's point of view. It is the ship's "staff" who provide the passenger contact. They include the chief purser, who is in charge of currency exchange and other money matters; the cruise director and a team of assistants who oversee shipboard social activities and entertainment; and the shore excursion director. Larger ships may have a hotel manager to oversee the dining and housekeeping functions. Otherwise, these responsibilities lie with the chief steward, who is head of the catering and restaurant facilities and is assisted by the *maître d'hôtel* in the dining room. The chief housekeeper marshals the cabin stewards and stewardesses and organizes laundry and cleaning services.

Dining and table allocations

In addition to informal self-service eating areas on board ship, all three main meals of the day are served in the more formal dining room. However, seating allocations are usually only made for the evening meal. You should be able to specify whether you would prefer the early or late sitting, a table in the smoking or nonsmoking section, the size of the table, and any special dietary requirements. If you are unhappy with your allotted table, ask the *maître d'hôtel* to move you.

Spending money

Most cruise lines include in the price of your ticket five meals a day (alcoholic drinks excluded), room service, live entertainment, and the use of facilities such as the health club and library. However, remember to budget for additional expenses, such as shore excursions, bar bills, laundry, and staff tips at the end of the cruise (see pages 188–9).

Land ahoy!

Emerging from the air-conditioned comfort of your cruise ship onto a bustling Caribbean dockside can be a bit of a shock in more ways than one. First, there's the heat – so make sure you are comfortably dressed for it. Second, there may be a sea of seemingly predatory taxi drivers and hawkers clamoring for your attention. This is not meant to be as intimidating as it seems. A smile and a firm "no thank you" is a far more potent crowd dissolver than bluster and outrage.

You may, on the other hand, need the services of a taxi driver. Getting around the islands in a limited period of time can be a problem, and the answer is generally a knowledgeable local driver. Before you take a taxi, check out the government or tourist office recommended rates for trips to various popular destinations. They are usually posted in the local tourist office, in information booths, or on the dockside itself. This way, you can fix the fare in advance, and be sure you are paying a fair rate.

Disembarking from the *Monarch of the Seas* and *Horizon* at St. John's, Antigua

There may be plenty of hustle and bustle on the streets, but Caribbean islanders are *never* in a hurry. "Re-l-a-a-a-x" is the motto hereabouts, and there is always time for a friendly greeting before any business gets done. This is no place for getting uptight, so down shift a gear or two and enjoy the laid-back attitude. But do not lose sight of your valuables. Though there is little danger of violent crime on most islands, petty theft is a constant irritant.

SEA SICKNESS

Sea sickness is nowadays a rare occurence owing to highly effective ships' stabilizers and the Caribbean's usual glassy-calm, but it is still a possibility for a few unlucky cruisers. Over-the-counter tablets, such as Dramamine, are available from the ship's stores. Consult the ship's doctor if the queasy feeling continues, or if you are taking other medication. Some motion sickness sufferers prefer acupressure wristbands to drugs. For a mild case, take a walk on deck in the fresh air and focus on a fixed point, such as the horizon.

WHAT TO SEE

"I was altogether unprepared for
their beauty and grandeur."
CHARLES KINGSLEY,
*At Last, a Christmas in the
West Indies, 1871*

Greater Miami

*C*ruise port "Capital of the World" and gateway to the Caribbean, Miami is a cosmopolitan oceanfront city just a day-trip away from the sunny Bahama islands. It is a lively, modern metropolis, full of contrasts, cultural diversity, and a whole host of tourist attractions and activities.

Tourism in Miami began with the arrival of Henry Flagler's railroad in 1896. Florida folklore tells how Yankee pioneer Julia Tuttle intrigued Flagler by sending him fresh Miami orange blossom untouched by the Great Frost of 1894–5, which destroyed citrus groves as far south as Palm Beach. Flagler recognized the tourism potential of such a mild climate, extended his railroad south and thus founded modern Miami.

During the early years of the century, a handful of wealthy visitors established winter homes along the shore of Biscayne Bay. The grandest of these is James Deering's magnificent Vizcaya. Then, inspired by the 1920s Florida land boom, George Merrick laid out America's first planned community, Coral Gables, which remains some of the most sought-after real estate in town. Meanwhile, a failed offshore avocado plantation was anchored to the mainland by causeways and transformed into legendary Miami Beach.

Today, tourism is the city's number one industry, with about 11 million visitors a year. And around 3 million of these visitors will sail off into the sunset on board one of the 20 or so cruise ships that call the Port of Miami home.

Greater Miami covers a vast area of about 2,040 square miles. At its heart the skyscrapers of Downtown Miami's business district provide a futuristic skyline. But surprising pockets of early 20th-century charm also exist within the sprawling metropolis. These unexpected treats are often referred to as "the neighborhoods." The most famous is the pastel-painted Art Deco District on Miami Beach. Mainland Coconut Grove exudes a Bohemian air; while neighboring Coral Gables boasts Mediterranean-style architecture, country clubs, and tree-shaded avenues. For local color, look no further than the bustling Cuban district of Little Havana; or discover the Caribbean-Creole influences in Little Haiti. However, a word of warning: after dark, the Downtown business district is not recommended for wandering tourists; nor is Little Haiti.

> **Greater Miami Convention & Visitors Bureau** – 701 Brickell Avenue, Suite 2700, Miami, FL 33131. Tel: (305) 539 3093.

Miami's glittering Downtown skyline

MIAMI

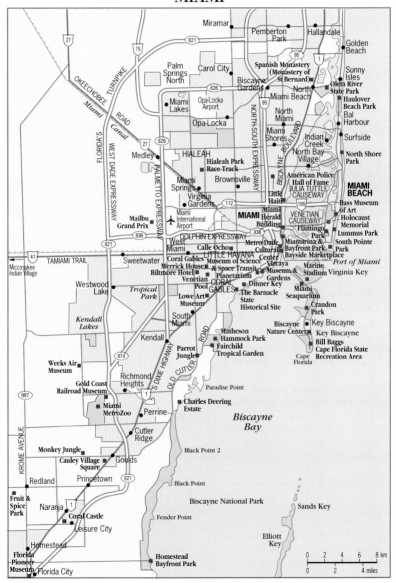

Pastel-painted Art Deco buildings on Ocean Drive provide a splash of color

ART DECO DISTRICT

The world's largest collection of Art Deco architecture, comprising some 800 individual buildings within a 1-square-mile area on Miami Beach. Ocean Drive is the center of the action – a favorite backdrop for photographic fashion shoots, café society, and evening strolls past spectacular neon-lit hotel façades (see pages 30–1).

Maps, information, and guided walking tours from the Art Deco Welcome Center, 1001 Ocean Drive, Miami Beach. Tel: (305) 672 2014. Open: Monday to Friday, 11am–6pm; Saturday, 10am–10pm; Sunday 11am–10pm.

AMERICAN POLICE HALL OF FAME

More than 10,000 law enforcement-related items give the inside scoop on American crime and punishment: police vehicles, weapons, jail cells, and an electric chair. Visitors are invited to solve a "homicide" at a mock-up crime scene.

3801 Biscayne Boulevard, north of Downtown. Tel: (305) 573 0070. Open: daily, 10am–5:30pm. Admission charge.

BASS MUSEUM OF ART

A first-class permanent collection of Old Master paintings, sculpture, furniture, and decorative arts is augmented by a wide-ranging calendar of special exhibitions.

2121 Park Avenue, Miami Beach. Tel: (305) 673 7530. Open: Tuesday to Saturday, 10am–5pm; Sunday, 1–5pm. Admission charge.

BAYFRONT PARK

A 32-acre open space on the Biscayne bayfront offering great views of the cruise ships, a concert amphitheater, jogging paths, and the John F. Kennedy Memorial Torch of Friendship – symbolizing Miami's ties to Latin America.

100 Biscayne Boulevard, Downtown (adjacent to Bayside Marketplace).

BAYSIDE MARKETPLACE

This lively shopping, entertainment, and dining complex overlooks the yachts in Miamarina. Browse around the 150 or so stores and the craft market, sample international cuisine, enjoy the antics of the street performers, and tune in to the daily concerts.

Bayside is accessible from the Port of Miami by Water Taxi service which serves the downtown area and Miami Beach (see box).

401 North Biscayne Boulevard. Tel: (305) 577 3344. Open: Monday to Thursday, 10am–10pm; Friday and Saturday, 10am–11pm; Sunday, 11am–8pm; extended hours in restaurants, bars, and cafés.

BILL BAGGS CAPE FLORIDA STATE RECREATION AREA

This natural preserve at the tip of Key Biscayne has been planted with native South Florida trees, and its mile-long sandy beach is one of the best spots on the bayfront. You'll find snack bars and barbecue areas, plus bicycles, snorkeling gear and fishing tackle for rent.

1200 South Crandon Boulevard, Key Biscayne. Tel: (305) 361 5811. Open: daily, 8am–sunset. Admission charge.

BISCAYNE NATURE CENTER

The center offers a hands-on look at southeast Florida's natural history. Call ahead for details of coastal hammock hikes, beach walks, bike and canoe trips, and local history lectures.

4000 Crandon Boulevard, Key Biscayne. Tel: (305) 556 7320. Call ahead for reservations and tour information.

CORAL CASTLE

A 20-year labor of love, this truly bizarre 1,100-ton carved coral-rock edifice was built single-handedly by lovesick Latvian Edward Leedskalnin, and is said to be a memorial to the sweetheart who jilted him. It includes coral rock furniture, solar-heated bathtubs, and a 9-ton gate.

28655 South Dixie Highway, Homestead. Tel: (305) 248 6344. Open: daily, 9am–6pm. Admission charge.

Entertainment on the quayside at Bayside Marketplace

WATER TAXIS

Miami's Water Taxi service is a neat way to get around the downtown area and Miami Beach. The downtown shuttle stops off at such key hotel, shopping and dining locations as the Biscayne Marriott, the Port of Miami, Bayside Market place, Brickell Key, and the Hyatt Regency.

The Miami Beach Marina stop is convenient for Ocean Drive; and there is also a stop for the trendy Lincoln Road Mall shopping district. *Services operate daily from noon. Tel: toll-free (954) 467 6677.*

CORAL GABLES MERRICK HOUSE

The Merrick family home takes its name from its Spanish-style roof tiles made from local coral. Coral Gables's founder, George Merrick, spent his teens here, and many of the furnishings and artifacts are genuine family pieces. The pretty gardens have been planted with a variety of native shrubs, scented jasmine, and fruit trees.

907 Coral Way, Coral Gables. Tel: (305) 460 5361. Open: Wednesday, 1–4pm (guided tours); gardens daily until sunset. Admission charge.

Tropical and subtropical plants surround George Merrick's former home

FAIRCHILD TROPICAL GARDEN

This is claimed to be the largest botanical gardens in the continental U.S., including 83 acres of tropical plants, rolling lawns, and clear lakes. Narrated tram tours give an overview of the grounds, and visitors are invited to explore special rainforest, mangrove, and Everglades areas, as well as the rare plant house.

10901 Old Cutler Road, Coral Gables. Tel: (305) 667 1651. Open: daily, 9:30am–4:30pm. Admission charge.

FRUIT AND SPICE PARK

There is a distinctly international flavor to this exotic 20-acre site. More than 500 varieties of fruits, nuts, spices, and herbs are cultivated here, many of them on sale in the gift shop.

24801 SW 187th Avenue, Homestead. Tel: (305) 247 5727. Open: daily, 10am–5pm. Admission charge.

GOLD COAST RAILROAD MUSEUM

This collection of historic locomotives, rolling stock (including a presidential pullman car used by presidents Roosevelt, Truman, Eisenhower, Reagan, and Bush), and railroad memorabilia is just the ticket for train buffs. Train rides are a weekend highlight.

12450 SW 152nd Street, Kendall. Tel: (305) 253 0063. Open: daily, 10am–3pm. Admission charge.

HAULOVER BEACH PARK

A 2-mile stretch of natural dunes and seashore, offering excellent facilities, including picnic areas, a children's playground, boat rental, walking trails, and tennis courts.

10800 Collins Avenue, North Miami Beach. Tel: (305) 947 3525.

LOWE ART MUSEUM

The exceptional and beautifully displayed Kress Collection of Renaissance and baroque art is the highlight of this elegant, small museum. It also features Spanish masterpieces, 19th- to 20th-century American works, Chinese porcelain, plus Asian, South American, and Native American artifacts among its treasures.
1301 Stanford Drive, Coral Gables. Tel: (305) 284 3535. Open: Tuesday, Wednesday, Friday and Saturday, 10am–5pm; Thursday, noon–7pm; Sunday, noon–5pm. Admission charge.

Art works in the Lowe Art Museum

METRO-DADE CULTURAL CENTER

A landmark cultural center that houses a trio of municipal showcases: the Miami Art Museum of Dade County, which focuses on Western art pre-1945; the state-of-the-art County Library; and the admirable Historical Museum of Southern Florida. At the latter, life-sized dioramas depict 10,000 years of local history with the help of artifacts and hands-on displays.
101 W Flagler Street, Downtown. Tel: Art Museum – (305) 375 1700; Historical Museum – (305) 375 1492. Open: Monday to Saturday (except Art Museum-closed Monday), 10am–5pm (Thursdays until 9pm); Sunday, noon–5pm. Admission charge.

MIAMI METROZOO

This is one of the largest "cageless" zoos in the U.S., housing more than 1,000 animals. Natural habitats have been created to simulate the African veldt and jungle forests, and a 2-mile monorail circuit ensures a bird's-eye view of the residents. Highlights include a walk-through aviary, rare white Bengal tigers, and a range of appealing animal shows.
12400 SW 152nd Street, South Miami. Tel: (305) 251 0400. Open: daily, 9:30am–5:30pm. Admission charge.

MIAMI SEAQUARIUM

A fun outing for all the family, the Seaquarium combines an educational look at the marine world with exciting shows. Check out the manatee reserve exhibit, dip into the touch tanks, watch the shark feeding, and take your seats for Lolita the orca whale, TV star Flipper the dolphin, and the comical Salty the Sea Lion Show.
4400 Rickenbacker Causeway. Tel: (305) 361 5705. Open: daily, 9:30am; closing times vary by season. Admission charge.

Dolphins at the Miami Seaquarium

ARCHITECTURAL EXTRAVAGANZAS

Enthusiastic developers have long believed that anything is possible in Miami. Architects inspired by the vision of wide blue skies, exotic palm trees, and balmy temperatures have been positively encouraged to let their imaginations run wild. A happy result of this is that, in addition to the famous Art Deco District (see page 22), Miami is home to many other splendid and bizarre examples of 20th-century architecture.

Take, for instance, James Deering's Vizcaya (see page 29). A short drive from the sheer glass and steel monuments to high finance of Brickell Avenue, this lavish 70-room Italianate villa, completed in 1918, is one of the earliest examples of the Miami building boom. No expense was spared, and it is said that the roof tiles once covered an entire Cuban village.

Italian-style Vizcaya (above);
Spanish-style Puerto del Sol (below)

Towering monuments: the Biltmore Hotel (above) and the Freedom Tower (right)

Spanish-Mediterranean was the preferred style for Coral Gables, George Merrick's "City Beautiful," founded in 1921. Among the special features here is the grand Puerto del Sol entrance, the enchanting Venetian Pool (see page 29), and Merrick's pet project, The Villages. These seven enclaves of distinctive vernacular architecture range in style from Chinese and Italian to Dutch Colonial (see pages 32–3). The 300-foot Spanish tower atop the imposing 1925 Biltmore Hotel is a local landmark, and the hotel swimming pool is the largest in the U.S., a magnificent L-shaped affair, edged by colonnades.

Another themed community was Glenn Curtiss' Opa-Locka, a 1926 Moorish-style development in North Miami. Drawing inspiration from *1,001 Tales from the Arabian Nights*, Curtiss' architect was instructed to lay out streets in the shape of a crescent moon, to name them after characters from the book, and to adorn buildings (from the railway station to the City Hall) with all manner of Moorish domes, minarets, and painted tiles.

On a more classical note, elegant Hialeah Park is one of the most beautiful horse-racing courses in the world, with its ivy-covered French-style clubhouse, completed in 1932. The eye-catching blue-and-white tiled façade of the Bacardi Imports Building, 2100 Biscayne Boulevard, also dates from the 1930s, while farther south on the same street the Freedom Tower strikes a surprise Old World note on the Downtown skyline. It was built in 1925 for the *Miami News* as a copy of the Giralda Tower in Seville, Spain. Later, it was used to process Cuban refugees; hence, the name.

MICCOSUKEE INDIAN VILLAGE AND AIRBOAT TOURS

This is a chance for visitors to catch a glimpse of the "traditional" Miccosukee Indian way of life – now sadly commercialized to something of a sideshow. Demonstrations of native crafts and alligator wrestling take place, and there is a museum, as well as a restaurant serving Miccosukee-inspired food. From here, you can also explore the Everglades by airboat.
Mile Marker 70, Tamiami Trail, 30 miles west of downtown on US41. Tel: (305) 223 8380. Open: daily, 9am–5pm. Admission charge.

Not just a pretty face: Parrot Jungle residents take part in daily shows

MONKEY JUNGLE

In 1933, animal behaviorist Joe Dumond released six macaque monkeys in a 10-acre hardwood hammock intending to study their habits. However, running short of funds, he caged in walkways for visitors and the free-ranging macaque colony developed into a popular attraction. Now, around 500 primates (mostly caged) represent 50 species of monkeys, and regular shows are staged.
14805 SW 216th Street, Homestead.

Tel: (305) 235 1611. Open: daily, 9:30am–5pm. Admission charge.

MIAMI MUSEUM OF SCIENCE & SPACE TRANSIT PLANETARIUM

This is a gripping voyage of exploration through the mysteries of science and space enlivened by more than 140 hands-on displays, multimedia shows, robotic dinosaurs, virtual reality basketball and a planetarium (tel: (305) 854 2222 for schedules). Natural history exhibits include an outdoor Wildlife Center that rehabilitates injured birds.
3280 South Miami Avenue, Coconut Grove. Tel: (305) 854 4247. Open: daily, 10am–6pm. Admission charge.

PARROT JUNGLE & GARDENS

Parrot Jungle's brightly colored cast of more than 1,000 exotic birds is due to move to Watson Island, off Miami Beach, in 1999. The new subtropical garden site will include enclosures for alligators, chimps, and giant tortoises. Meanwhile, the parrot shows and famous pink flamingos continue to appear in South Miami.
11000 SW 57th Avenue, South Miami. Tel: (305) 666 7834. Open: daily, 9:30am–6pm. Admission charge.

SPANISH MONASTERY

Strange but true, Miami is the unlikely site of the oldest building in the U.S. Newspaper magnate William Randolph Hearst bought the 12th-century cloisters of St. Bernard's Monastery and shipped them from Segovia, Spain, in 1929. Re-erected in 1954, they now serve as an Episcopal church.
16711 West Dixie Highway, North Miami Beach. Tel: (305) 945 1462. Open: guided tours Monday to Saturday, 10am–4pm; Sunday, noon–4pm. Admission charge.

In 1926, the Venetian Pool was drained to host a performance by the Miami Opera

VENETIAN POOL

This Venetian-inspired lagoon, complete with little hump-backed bridges, grottoes, and waterfalls (all carved out of an old coral rock quarry), is one of the most unusual and delightful swimming pools imaginable. In its heyday, the Miami Opera, *Tarzan* star Johnny Weissmuller, and bathing belle Esther Williams all performed here. Now visitors can bask on the sandy beach, bathe in the crystal-clear water fed by a natural spring, and find refreshments in the courtyard café. *2701 De Soto Boulevard, Coral Gables. Tel: (305) 460 5356. Open: Tuesday to Friday, 11am–5:30pm; weekends, 10am–4:30pm. Admission charge.*

VIZCAYA MUSEUM AND GARDENS

Built as a winter home for industrialist James Deering between 1916 and 1918, this palatial Italian Renaissance-style villa is one of Miami's finest attractions. It is set back from Biscayne Bay, on 10 acres of formal landscaped gardens, and acts as a showcase for Deering's treasure trove of 15th- to 19th-century antiques. Each of the thirty-four rooms is devoted to a different style and period, including a Renaissance Hall, a classical 18th-century English Adam's-style Library, and a magnificent rococo Salon. *3251 South Miami Avenue, Coconut Grove. Tel: (305) 250 9133. Open: daily, 9:30am–5pm (gardens 5:30pm). Admission charge.*

WEEKS AIR MUSEUM

The history of aviation up to 1945 is illustrated by a notable collection of 35 restored historic aircraft, plus scale models, memorabilia, and video displays. *Tamiami Airport, 14710 SW 128th Street, Kendall. Tel: (305) 233 5197. Open: daily, 10am–5pm. Admission charge.*

Art Deco District

In 1915, John Collins borrowed $50,000 and began to develop Miami Beach. As the mangrove wilderness was cleared, gardens were landscaped, shopping malls and sports facilities took shape, and the first homes and hotels appeared, many in the popular 1920s Mediterranean Revival-style. After a brief hiatus during the Depression years, Miami Beach emerged as a showcase for the dashing new Art Deco architects of the 1930s and 1940s. A new generation of Streamlined Moderne buildings, with their sweeping curves and smooth planes, reflected the contemporary preoccupation with futurism and enthusiasm for the aerodynamic age. Rescued from decay in the 1970s, today's rejuvenated Art Deco District is one of the world's most fashionable places. *Allow 3 hours.*

Start on Ocean Drive at 6th Street. Stroll up to the Art Deco Welcome Center.

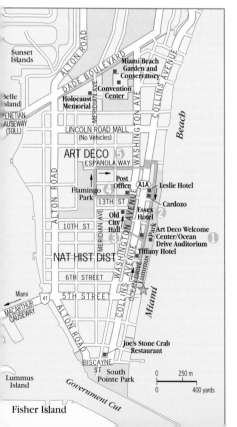

1 OCEAN DRIVE

Facing the ocean across Lummus Park and the beach, Ocean Drive unfurls in a magnificent sweep of Art Deco delights: streamline façades, bold vertical planes, racing stripes, "eyebrow" windows, and nautical and geometric motifs. The Park Central (No. 630) employs all manner of these deco devices. Also note the name-sake neon-lit tower atop the Waldorf (No. 860), and ship's prow on the Breakwater (No. 940), which shares a pool with the Mediterranean-Revival Edison (No. 960). *Stop at the Welcome Center (see page 22) for information and maps; then head away from the beach on 10th Street.*

2 ESSEX HOTEL

A short walk down 10th Street leads to the Essex Hotel, with an etched glass flamingo on the porch door. Opposite, the Fairmont Hotel boasts extravagant

Palm trees and candy-striped awnings shade shoppers on Espanola Way

neon. The huge Washington Storage Building (1001 Washington Avenue), with its window grilles and Spanish baroque-style carved reliefs, is now home to the Wolfsonian Foundation, which exhibits decorative and propaganda arts. *Turn right onto Washington Avenue.*

3 WASHINGTON AVENUE
Just north on Washington Avenue, there is a clutch of modest 1930s hotels: the Washingon Park, Taft, and Kenmore (Nos. 1020, 1044, 1050). The 1927 Old City Hall (No. 1130) is a nine-story Mediterranean affair decorated with giant urns. Take a moment to visit the Depression Moderne-style Post Office (No. 1300). Its rotunda has a mural and painted ceiling above the semicircle of original brass mailboxes.
This is a bit of a detour, but interesting if you have time. Walk west on 13th Street, north on Meridian Avenue, and return east on Espanola Way.

4 APARTMENT BUILDINGS
On 13th Street, pretty Chrisken Court (No. 541) features hefty wooden balconies and decorative reliefs. The Parkway Apartments, on the corner of Meridian Avenue, enjoy a balconied courtyard, colorful tiled steps, and niches filled with urns. The upper section of Spanish-themed, gas-lit Espanola Way has several restored apartment houses, such as the simple Streamlined Allen (No. 609–611) and Mediterranean (No. 531–525).

5 ESPANOLA WAY
From Drexel Avenue, William Whitman's 1922 Spanish Village runs for a block east on Espanola Way. The tree-shaded sidewalks are lined with cafés, boutiques, jewelers, and retro dealers selling second-hand clothes and antiques beneath a cheerful array of striped awnings and balconies. Take a break here before returning to the top end of Ocean Drive.
Cross Washington Avenue, opposite the Cameo Cinema (a model of Streamlined Vitralite). On the corner of Collins Avenue, turn left by the former Hoffman's Caféteria (No. 1450), with its distinctive cut-out corner façade. Take the first right, and rejoin Ocean Drive.

Wolfsonian Foundation – open:
Tuesday to Saturday, 10am–6pm;
Sunday, noon–5pm; admission charge.

Coconut Grove and Coral Gables

Coconut Grove is one of Miami's oldest and most attractive neighborhoods. It is a good place to begin this 10-mile jaunt, which includes a detour around Coral Gables, the Fairchild Tropical Garden, and a swimming opportunity. *Make a day of it; pack a picnic.*

From Grand Avenue, opposite Cocowalk, take Main Highway south.

1 COCONUT GROVE

There were only two coconut palms in the "grove" when Horace P. Porter opened his Post Office, in 1873. Early visitors to the area

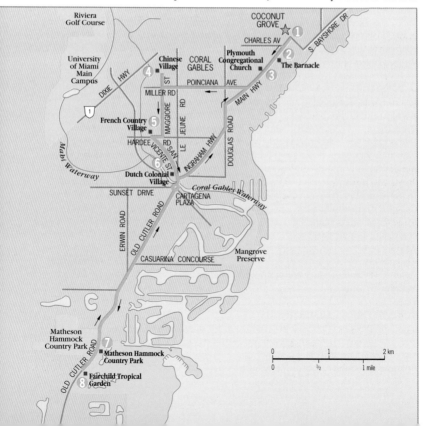

stayed in rustic cabins along the shore. Today, the sidewalks may be brick and the streetlamps Victorian, but the Grove is hip and happening. Great shopping and good restaurants abound. On the corner of Charles Avenue, where 19th-century Bahamanian immigrants built traditional wood-frame "conch" homes, the Spanish rococo-style Coconut Grove Playhouse is a leading theater venue.
Take Main Highway south.

2 THE BARNACLE

The Barnacle is a suitable name for a home designed by a naval architect. Ralph Middleton Munroe built this fine two-story house in 1891. It is set behind hardwood trees with lawns stretching down to a boathouse on the bay. The inspired period furnishings include paintings and photographs.
Continue on Main Highway.

3 PLYMOUTH CONGREGATIONAL CHURCH

This weathered stone church was designed in the style of a Spanish mission building. Its 400-year-old oak and walnut door came from the Pyrenees, and there is a quiet garden cloister around to the right.
Turn right on Poinciana Avenue; cross Le Jeune Road for Miller Road and the intersection with Maggiore Street. The Chinese Village is 4 blocks north (right) at Castania Avenue.

4, 5, AND 6 CORAL GABLES VILLAGES

A special feature of George Merrick's "City Beautiful," these small groups of houses are not villages in the real sense, and some only cover a single block. The tiny Chinese Village (4) features sweeping roofs in green, yellow, and

blue, cut-out oriental motifs, and bamboo-design window grilles. Take Maggiore Street south to Hardee Road and head one block west (right). The French Country Village (5) employs towers, pointed slate "witches-hat" roofs, and wooden shutters. Then head south on San Vicente Street. The pretty, whitewashed Dutch Colonial Village (6) is particularly striking with its gables, red-tiled roofs and twisted barley sugar chimneys etched against a deep blue sky.
Go south on Le Jeune Road to Cartagena Plaza; then south on Old Cutler Road.

7 MATHESON HAMMOCK COUNTRY PARK

A terrific bayside park with a beach (including shower and changing facilities), picnic tables, refreshments, walking trails, and bike paths among the mangroves.
Continue south on Old Cutler Road.

8 FAIRCHILD TROPICAL GARDEN

Beautiful tropical gardens full of colorful blooms, exotic plants, and rustling palms (see page 24).
Return to Cartagena Plaza. Head north to the traffic lights on Le Jeune Road and then right onto Ingraham Highway to rejoin Main Highway and return to Coconut Grove.

The Barnacle – 3485 Main Highway, Coconut Grove. Tel: (305) 448 9445. Open: guided tours Friday to Sunday, 10am, 11:30am, 1pm, and 2:30pm. Admission charge.
Matheson Hammock Country Park – 9610 Old Cutler Road, Coral Gables. Tel: (305) 667 3035. Open: daily, 8am–sunset. Admission charge for cars.

Fort Lauderdale

*A*n hour's journey north of Miami, Fort Lauderdale is one of Florida's leading beach resorts, and its five-star cruise facility, Port Everglades, serves over 2½ million cruise passengers each year.

Fort Lauderdale is all glitter, from the tips of its Downtown skyscrapers to the maze of sparkly waterways which have earned it the nickname the "Venice of America." It is a brash but friendly Gold Coast success story and is one of the fastest growing cities in the state.

The first settlers

The city is named after Major William Lauderdale, who established the first of three small forts here in the 1830s. In 1893, pioneer settler Frank Stranahan established an overnight camp for the Bay Biscayne Stage Coach Line and traded provisions for alligator hides, pelts, and egret plumes brought to him by the local Seminole Indians. With the arrival of the railroad in 1896, a small settlement grew around the trading post and attracted the attention of Florida State Governor Napoleon Bonaparte Broward, who unveiled what would have been an environmentally disastrous plan to drain the Everglades.

Dredging operations began along the

The emphasis in Fort Lauderdale is firmly on its waterfront

New River in 1906. Then, during the 1920s, a Venetian landbuilding technique, known as "finger-islanding," was used to transform the mangrove swamps between the river and the Intracoastal Waterway into a network of channels and building plots.

Today, the city's 300 miles of navigable inland waterways are one of its top attractions, plied by boats, yachts, and water taxis.

Golden opportunities

From the 1950s through to the 1970s, Fort Lauderdale was infamous for its raucous spring break student parties. However, following a clamp-down by the authorities, the students have moved on and the city has emerged as a popular year-round family tourist destination.

Together with its neighboring

FORT LAUDERDALE

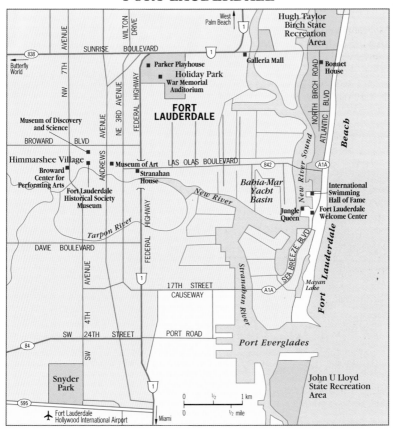

beachside communities, Greater Fort Lauderdale offers 23 miles of golden beaches, historic homes, modern museums, fine shopping, and a range of family attractions. Top-class facilities, such as the magnificent Broward Center for the Performing Arts, complement the city's culturally dynamic community.

For outdoor types, there are sporting opportunities galore, including golf, diving, sailing, sportfishing, and tennis.

Spectators can enjoy fast and furious sports, such as jai-alai (a version of the Basque *pelota* involving a small ball being hurled at speeds of up to 175mph with the aid of curved wicker slings attached to players' hands) at Dania, thoroughbred racing at Gulfstream Park, and weekly rodeos in Davie. Meanwhile, baseball fans can catch the Baltimore Orioles spring training at Fort Lauderdale's Yankee Stadium.

BONNET HOUSE

This lovely plantation-style house is set in a leafy 36-acre estate, just a stone's throw from the Downtown skyscrapers. Artists Frederick Clay Bartlett and his wife, Evelyn, designed the eclectic and unusual interior with a rich collection of decorative and fine arts. Namesake bonnet lilies grow around a miniature lake in the grounds. *900 N Birch Road. Tel: (954) 563 5393. Open: guided tours only, Wednesday to Friday, 10am and 1pm; Saturday and Sunday, 1pm and 2pm. Admission charge.*

Butterfly World – a lush indoor tropical rain forest housing thousands of butterflies

BUTTERFLY WORLD

This popular attraction provides a dazzling insight into the insect world. Around 100 species of butterflies inhabit huge walk-through aviaries, planted with tropical foilage. There's also a butterfly-breeding center, an insectarium, and a museum. *Tradewinds Park South, 3600 W Sample Road, Coconut Creek. Tel: (954) 977 4400. Open: Monday to Saturday, 9am–5pm; Sunday, 1–5pm.*

SOUTH FLORIDA TROLLEY TOURS AND WATER TAXIS

Here are two great ways to get around Fort Lauderdale and see the sights. South Florida Trolley Tours offers daily narrated historical tours in old San Francisco-style trams with pickups from all major hotels (tel: (954) 429 3100 for information).

Fort Lauderdale's water taxis navigate the Intracoastal Waterway and New River, with stops at a variety of waterside locations from shopping centers to restaurants and attractions. The service operates daily from 10am, and offers at a set one-way fare, or you can buy a good value day-pass. Pick up a taxi from the dock in the port, or call the operator (tel: (954) 467 6677) and make a booking.

EVERGLADES HOLIDAY PARK AIRBOAT TOURS

Skim across the shallow marshes on an airboat for a real Everglades experience, which includes a visit to a replica Seminole Indian village and views of Southern Florida's unique flora and fauna. *21940 Griffin Road. Tel: (954) 434 8111. Open: daily, tours every 30 minutes from 9am–5pm.*

FLAMINGO GARDENS

One of the area's earliest citrus groves has been transformed into a splendid garden, bursting with exotic blooms and towering trees, and inhabited by a collection of animals and birds, including monkeys, crocodiles, alligators, and, of course, flamingos. A tram ride explores the 60-acre site, which also offers a petting zoo, museum, and store.

Flamingo Gardens combines botanic gardens with a children's zoo and, of course, flamingos

rabbits, and wading birds. A short film show at the Visitor Center gives a history and introduction to the park.
3109 E Sunrise Boulevard. Tel: (954) 564 4521. Open: daily, 8am–dusk. Admission charge.

INTERNATIONAL SWIMMING HALL OF FAME AQUATIC COMPLEX

The Hall of Fame features a terrific array of swimming memorabilia in its museum wing. There are displays on all-time greats, such as Johnny "Tarzan" Weissmuller and Mark Spitz, plus Olympic gold medals, swimwear through the ages, and much more. The Aquatic Complex, with its two Olympic pools and diving facilities, is patronized by Olympic hopefuls, and it is also open to the public.
501 Seabreeze Boulevard. Tel: (954) 468 1580. Open: daily, 8am–4pm; and Monday to Friday 6–8pm. Admission charge.

3750 Flamingo Road, Davie. Tel: (954) 473 2955. Open: daily, 10am–6pm. Admission charge.

HUGH TAYLOR BIRCH STATE RECREATION AREA

A 180-acre green breathing space, locked between the beachfront and Intracoastal Waterway. Walk or drive around the 1¾-mile circuit, investigate the short beach hardwood hammock trail, or rent a canoe and keep an eye out for racoons, marsh

One of the Olympic-sized pools at the International Swimming Hall of Fame

Modern art on display outside Edward Larabee Barnes' stylish 1986 Museum of Art building

JUNGLE QUEEN

This old-style riverboat offers daily sightseeing cruises around the waterways of the "Venice of America." It glides past exclusive waterfront homes and stops off at a purpose-built Indian Village for a spot of alligator wrestling and souvenir shopping. At night, sail up the New River for a "Bar-B-Que & Shrimp Dinner Cruise" on a private island, an all-you-can-eat spread with entertainment in the form of a vaudeville show and an old-fashioned sing-along.

Bahia Mar Yacht Center (off A1A), Fort Lauderdale Beach. Tel: (954) 462 5596 for schedules and information.

LAS OLAS BOULEVARD AND HORSE AND CARRIAGE TOURS

Fort Lauderdale's prettiest shopping street is landscaped with flowers and trees, and studded with a host of chic designer boutiques, art and antiques galleries, and attractive restaurants.

When the traffic dies down in the early evening, Las Olas Horse and Carriage Tours offers romantic horse-drawn drives around the Downtown and Las Olas districts.

SE 8th Avenue and Las Olas Boulevard. Tel: (954) 763 7393. Tuesday to Sunday from 7pm.

MUSEUM OF ART

This state-of-the-art showcase is renowned for its fine collections of 19th- and 20th-century American and European paintings and sculpture. In addition, there are collections of ethnic art, and the gallery stages some interesting temporary exhibitions, including the M. Allen Hortt Memorial Competition, South Florida's top art prize (September to October). Drop in at the excellent museum store, too.

1 E Las Olas Boulevard, Downtown. Tel: (954) 525 5500. Open: Tuesday, 11am–9pm; Wednesday to Saturday, 10am–5pm; Sunday, noon–5pm. Admission charge.

MUSEUM OF DISCOVERY AND SCIENCE

A $30-million hands-on museum packed with marvellous gadgets, games, and educational exhibits that make learning lots of fun. There are seven display areas ranging from the hi-tech Space Base to the grassroots Florida

Getting to grips with a tarantula at the Museum of Discovery and Science

EcoScapes, with its walk-through guide to local habitats. Test your skill at Laser Pinball, take a space ride on the Manned Maneuvering Unit, or goggle in amazement at the five-story-high IMAX movie screen.

401 SW 2nd Street. Tel: (954) 467 6637. Open: Monday to Saturday, 10am–5pm; Sunday, noon–5pm. Admission charge.

RIVERWALK

The landscaped Riverwalk was part of the city's massive urban redesign program for the 1990s, and provides access to Fort Lauderdale's prime river frontage. Stroll along the New River from Stranahan House up to the historic Himmarshee Village area and Broward Center for the Performing Arts, stopping off to admire the views from an outdoor café, picnic table, or park bench.

STRANAHAN HOUSE

The oldest house in Broward County, this homely pioneer property was founded on the banks of the New River, in 1900. Trader Frank Stranahan and his school teacher wife, Ivy Cromatie, lived here and entertained East Coast railway baron Henry Flagler in the pine panelled living room. The interior has been restored in the style of 1913–15, with antique Victorian furniture and period pieces, together with photographs of Fort Lauderdale's early days.

335 E Las Olas Boulevard (at SE 6th Avenue). Tel: (954) 524 4736. Open: tours Wednesday to Saturday, 10am–4pm; Sunday 1–4pm. Admission charge.

Frank Stranahan's pioneer home on the banks of the New River, Fort Lauderdale

THE EVERGLADES

The Native Americans called it *pa-hay-okee*, or "grassy waters," a name later paraphrased by ecologist Marjorie Stoneman Douglas as the title of her evocative book *The Everglades: River of Grass*. It is an accurate description of this vast, water-logged region, which stretches from Lake Okeechobee in the north, down to Florida Bay and the Gulf of Mexico. The endless vista of rippling, razor-sharp sawgrass was once a hideout for Seminole Indians who traveled the maze of secret waterways. Now it is the last refuge of the rare Florida panther and a haven for other endangered species, such as the Everglades mink, American crocodile, roseate spoonbill, bald eagle, and osprey.

Airboat rides provide unparalleled access to Everglades waterways

The best time to visit the Everglades is during the dry, winter season. Wildlife spotting is easier as the animals and birds gather around the deep-water sloughs (waterholes) to feed, and there are fewer mosquitoes to trouble you. Over 2,000 plant species flourish in the subtropical conditions, and 45 of these are unique to the region. Rising above the marshy grasslands, shady hammocks (small woods) of willow, pine, and tropical hardwoods, such as mahogany and live oak, cling to limestone outcrops, providing shelter for wildlife and a host for airplants, orchids, and bromeliads. A less welcome guest is the parasitic strangler fig, dropping its tangled aerial roots to the ground and gradually depriving the host tree of water and light until it dies. Stands of elegant cypress trees are mirrored in the tannin-rich waters of quiet swamps.

The Everglades is itself endangered. Stoneman Douglas's book (written in 1947) was one of the first impassioned pleas to developers and politicians to preserve the fragile Everglades ecosystem. The crusade against its destruction continues today, despite the fact that the 1.4 million-acre Everglades National Park has been declared a World Heritage Site in recognition of its outstanding natural resources.

Everglades National Park is one of the world's most outstanding natural habitats

Key West

*T*he southernmost city in the United States, Key West is a popular stop with several cruise lines operating in the Caribbean. Measuring just 4 miles by 2 miles, Key West remains at heart a village (albeit a rather exotic one). It is a quirky mix of old and new, quiet tree-lined backstreets and hip café society, New World cuisine and old-style wooden "gingerbread" houses. Once the haunt of pirates and wreckers (more politely known as ship's salvagers), Key West is now a popular gay enclave, and welcomes the annual winter invasion of tourists with amused tolerance.

While walking is the best way to savor the charms and relaxed atmosphere of Old Key West (the central nub of town), you can also be ferried around the main island sights aboard the Old Town Trolley, or take a 90-minute narrated tour on the Conch Train. Should you be ashore at dusk, the sunset celebrations on Mallory Dock performed by a host of wacky street entertainers and musicians are a near-legendary institution.

AUDUBON HOUSE AND GARDENS

The famous naturalist and artist John James Audubon never actually stayed in this fine 1830 house. However, he worked on his paintings in the garden while visiting the island in 1832 to study the native birds.

205 Whitehead Street. Tel: (305) 294 2116. Open: daily, 9:30am–5pm.
Admission charge.

FORT ZACHARY TAYLOR STATE HISTORIC SITE

Founded in 1845, Fort Zachary Taylor was a rare Union outpost in the south during the Civil War. Rescued from obscurity, it now houses a small museum and a large collection of Civil War cannons. On the shore, there is a public beach with picnic tables in the shade.

Music in Mallory Square, Key West

Southard Street, in the Truman Annex. Tel: (305) 292 6713. Open: daily, 8am–dusk. Admission charge.

HEMINGWAY HOUSE

Ernest Hemingway moved into this mid-19th-century house in 1931 with his second wife, Pauline, and they furnished it with a mixture of Spanish, Cuban, and African mementoes of their travels. The author wrote most of his finest work here, and his eight-toed cats' descendants still have the run of the place. The entertaining guided tours impart a wealth of anecdotal information.
907 Whitehead Street. Tel: (305) 294 1575. Open: daily, 9am–5pm. Admission charge.

KEY WEST AQUARIUM

The aquarium has been a local attraction since 1932, offering aquariums, touch tanks, turtle pens, and shark feeding opportunities for fearless visitors.
1 Whitehead Street. Tel: (305) 296 2051. Open: daily, 10am–6pm. Admission charge.

KEY WEST LIGHTHOUSE MUSEUM

This 1848 lighthouse affords splendid views over Key West and the coast from its viewing balcony, reached by way of eighty-eight steps. There is an interesting small museum in the former Keeper's Quarters.
938 Whitehead Street. Tel: (305) 294 0012. Open: daily, 9:30am–5pm. Admission charge.

LITTLE WHITE HOUSE MUSEUM

President Harry S. Truman's "alternative White House" during his six years in office, this late 19th-century house has been restored in the style of the 1940s.

Spanish silver ingots on display at the Mel Fisher Maritime Heritage Society

111 Front Street, Truman Annex. Tel: (305) 294 9911. Open: daily, 9am–5pm. Admission charge.

MEL FISHER MARITIME HERITAGE MUSEUM

Gold bullion, fabulous jewelry, silver tableware, and other treasures salvaged from Spanish wrecks by Key West's most famous treasure hunter, Mel Fisher, are on display here. Start with the riveting video presentation, and end at the shop where souvenir replicas and genuine treasures are on sale.
200 Greene Street. Tel: (305) 294 2633. Open: daily, 9:30am–5pm. Admission charge.

WRECKER'S MUSEUM

Key West's oldest house, this 1829 sea captain's home evokes a distinctly nautical air. It contains period furnishings and a variety of artifacts, model ships, pictures, and documents relating to the 19th-century wrecking (salvage) industry.
322 Duval Street. Tel: (305) 294 9502. Open: daily, 10am–4pm. Admission charge.

Antigua

*T*he largest of the Leeward islands, Antigua (pronounced An-tee-ga) combines some of the finest white-sand beaches in the Caribbean with several interesting historical sites. The island was discovered by Christopher Columbus on his second voyage to the New World in 1493, and named after Santa Maria de la Antigua, a miraculous statue of the Virgin in Seville Cathedral. Its earliest inhabitants were Stone Age Siboney people who migrated from South America around 4,000 years ago. The Siboneys, and their successors, the Arawaks, left their mark on several Amerindian sites, especially around Indian Town. An English colony from St. Kitt's established the first permanent European settlement here in 1632, and, except for two brief periods of occupation by the French and Spanish, Antigua remained linked to Britain, until full Independence in 1981.

Antigua's scalloped, irregular coastline is one of its chief delights. They say there are 365 beaches – one for every day of the year. Fine natural harbors, such as St. John's, Falmouth, and English Harbour, have welcomed sailors for generations, and sailing is still big news on the island. The Caribbean's winter sailing calendar culminates in April/May with Antigua Race Week, a major international regatta and week-long party.

ST. JOHN'S

The entrance to St. John's Harbour is guarded by Fort Barrington and Fort

Looking out over English Harbour from Shirley Heights, Antigua

ANTIGUA

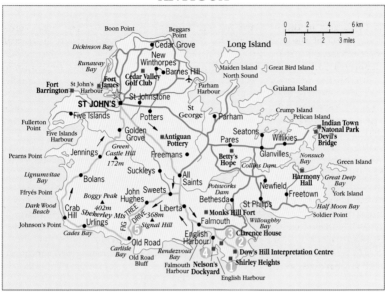

James, two of the numerous 18th-century defensive structures built by the British. Behind the forts, the attractive West Indian town climbs gently back from the wharf in a friendly jumble of clapboard houses, fretwork balconies, and roadside stalls to St John's Cathedral, flanked by its twin towers topped with silver cupolas. Erected in the mid-19th century on the site of two previous churches, the dignified wooden interior is worth a visit for its barrel ceilings supported by octagonal pillars, the decorative upper gallery, and grand memorials bedecked with coats-of-arms and purple prose.

Museum of Antigua and Barbuda

Housed in the Old Court House, built in 1750, this small museum traces the history of Antigua and its tiny island sister Barbuda, which were once joined together. Relics of the ancient Siboney and Arawak Indians include grinding stones, axe heads, and conch-shell chisels. There are sections on the plantation era and local flora and bird life, but pride of place goes to the cricket bat of former West Indian and Antiguan cricket captain Viv Richards.

Corner of Market and Long streets. Tel: (268) 462 1469. Open: Monday to Friday, 8:30am–4pm, Saturday 10am–2pm. Free.

Antigua Department of Tourism – PO Box 363, St. John's. Tel: (268) 462 0480. There is also a tourist information booth on the dock at Heritage Quay, St. John's.

Palm-fringed Dark Wood Beach on Antigua's southwest coast

DARK WOOD BEACH AND CRAB HILL

The Caribbean idyll – a crescent of soft, pale sand bordering clear, turquoise waters and fringed by palms – Dark Wood Beach is almost deserted during the week, but busy on the weekend. Good beach bars.

Farther south, Johnson's Point is another quiet sand strip on Crab Hill Bay. Look out for the shell-lined steps to The Nature of Things, a fantastic shell shop in Crab Hill Village. The interior is a veritable treasury of conch shells and coral, sea urchins, starfish, barracuda heads sporting marbles for eyes, loofahs,

Naval Officers' House in Nelson's Dockyard, English Harbour

and sponges perched on shelves, balanced on beams, and cradled in fishing nets.

DICKINSON BAY

Just north of St. John's, Fort James Beach is the closest beach to the capital, but many short-stay visitors prefer to head a little farther north to the resort area at Dickinson Bay. It provides silky sand, windsurfer and catamaran (Hobie Cat rental), plus a welcome choice of beach-side bars and restaurants in the shade.

ENGLISH HARBOUR AND FALMOUTH

One of the safest natural anchorages in the world, English Harbour was the British Admiralty's Caribbean base throughout the 18th and 19th centuries. The neighboring port of Falmouth was once the capital of Antigua, and the two bays, divided by a narrow isthmus fortified by the British, are busy yachting anchorages during the winter season.

Horatio Nelson was posted to English Harbour in 1784. The young captain of HMS *Boreas*, a twenty-eight-gun frigate, was not amused. He considered Antigua a "barbarous place," and fell out with the locals for enforcing the Navigation Act (banning trade with U.S. vessels) too vigorously. Angry businesspeople sued him for loss of earnings, and the future naval hero was forced to spend eight weeks on board his ship to avoid imprisonment. John Herbert of the Montpelier Plantation, Nevis (see page 117), put up Nelson's £10,000 bail, and when he went ashore to dine with his benefactor, Nelson met his wife-to-be, Fanny Nesbit. At the wedding, Fanny was given away by Nelson's friend Prince William Henry, later King William IV, who lived at Clarence House overlooking the harbor (see page 49).

Despite Nelson's aversion to the place, his name lingers on at Nelson's Dockyard, English Harbour's splendidly restored Georgian naval base in the Eastern Caribbean (see pages 48–9).
South coast, via All Saints.

THE NORTHEAST

If you want to explore far from the madding crowd, there are several pleasant spots dotted around the central and northeastern corner of the island.

Parham

In the middle of the north coast, Parham, a small fishing village with an unusual octagonal church, is one of the oldest settlements on Antigua.
Central north coast.

Betty's Hope

Betty's Hope was one of Antigua's chief 17th-century sugar plantations. Among the ruins, a stone windmill and its machinery have been restored and the visitors' center contains a small historical museum.
Off central island road to Indian Town. Open: Tuesday to Saturday, 10am–4pm. Admission charge.

Indian Town National Park

It's a scenic drive across the east coast and Indian Town National Park, where the Atlantic surf has carved blowholes and an impressive arch, known as Devil's Bridge, out of the limestone cliffs. This is a spectacular place on a blustery day.
Northeast coast.

Harmony Hall

This fine old stone house, built around a sugar mill, is a perfect spot for shopping and lunch, and you can even take a dip in their swimming pool. This is principally an art gallery selling the work of local artists and high quality Caribbean crafts. There is a breezy bar and lookout point in the old mill overlooking Nonsuch Bay.
East coast. Open: daily, 10am–6pm. Free.

Sugar mill relics

Exploring the Southern Coast

A great day out that takes in English Harbour, scenic Fig Tree Drive, and a chance to visit one of Antigua's most beautiful beaches, this tour can be accomplished either in a long morning, or at a more relaxing pace with a stop for lunch in Nelson's Dockyard (see map on page 45). *Allow 4 to 6 hours.*

From St. John's, take the road to English Harbour, via All Saints and Liberta. Drive past the turn-off for English Harbour and continue up to Shirley Heights.

1 SHIRLEY HEIGHTS

Named for General Sir Thomas Shirley, Governor of the Leeward Islands between 1781 and 1791, the fortified hills above English Harbour afford a magnificent view over the sheltered bays and across to the island of Guadeloupe. Remains of the 18th-century signals station, which could give advance warning of a French attack, and the once sizeable military complex are scattered over a large area. In the former Guard House (built 1791), a bar and restaurant hosts a popular Sunday brunch party with live music and a lively crowd.
Drive down to Dow's Hill.

Pillars in the garden of the Admiral's Inn

2 DOW'S HILL INTERPRETATION CENTRE

Start off in the modern Interpretation Centre with a 15-minute sound and light show depicting scenes from Antiguan history. The multimedia presentation traces the island's settlement by South American Indians, through the European Age of Discovery and Plantation era to the present day. Then step outside to enjoy views from the look-out point, perched on the ruins of the Belvedere, the 18th-century governor's residence. *Continue to Clarence House.*

3 CLARENCE HOUSE

Off the road leading down from Shirley Heights to Nelson's Dockyard, Clarence House was built for Prince William Henry, Duke of Clarence (later William IV of England) in 1786. Damaged by the hurricane in 1995, the house is closed for restoration, but remains the official country residence of the Governor-General. In the past, distinguished guests have included Sir Winston Churchill, and honeymooners Princess Margaret and Lord Snowdon. *Drive on to Nelson's Dockyard.*

4 NELSON'S DOCKYARD

Abandoned by the British Navy in 1889, this small Georgian dockyard was rescued from the doldrums in the 1960s, and restored to its present spick and span state of grey-shuttered stone and wooden buildings. Today, it bustles with yachtspeople and tourists.

Just inside the gates, a former pitch, tar, and turpentine store has been transformed into the Admiral's Inn, a small hotel. The sixteen massive pillars in its gardens once supported a sail loft: Boats would berth in the narrow dock below while their sails were pulled up into an overhead loft for repair. At the Nelson Museum in the Admiral's House (though no admiral stayed here), among the model ships and naval memorabilia, period prints depict Nelson's man-of-war-style funeral carriage, and the old cookhouse is now a bakery. An attractive brick building flanked by rounded cisterns used to store water, the Copper & Lumber Store Hotel sleeps guests in rooms named after famous naval battles and are served lunchtime snacks in the Mainbrace Pub. The open-sided Working Mast House is still in use today, while the former 1821 Officers' Quarters now house galleries selling contemporary crafts, reproduction prints, and old maps.
Retrace your journey along the All Saints road. Shortly after Liberta, turn left for Sweets and Old Road.

Dow's Hill Interpretation Centre –
open: daily, 9am–5pm. Admission charge.
Clarence House – closed until further notice.
Nelson's Dockyard – open: daily, exhibits 9am–5pm. Admission charge.

5 FIG TREE DRIVE

A rare corner of natural vegetation that escaped the 17th- and 18th-century sugarcane boom, this lovely palm-lined road is the most scenic on the island and winds through the forest and banana trees down to the coast.
Head west along the coast, pass Dark Wood Beach (see page 46), and return to St. John's.

The Bahamas

*O*n October 12, 1492, Christopher Columbus discovered the New World. He is said to have made landfall on the Bahamanian island of Guanahani, which he named San Salvador. North and east of the Caribbean proper, the 700 islands and 2,000-plus cays that comprise the Bahama Islands lie scattered across 100,000 square miles of Atlantic Ocean. Only about 30 of the islands are inhabited. Originally, the archipelago was named the Lucayans after the local Arawak people; "Bahamas" comes from the Spanish *baja-mar*, meaning "shallow sea."

These flat, barren coral rock islands were ignored by the Spanish and claimed by the British, who under the leadership of William Sayle, founded a Puritan settlement on Eleuthera in 1648. This initial settlement was a failure, but Sayle discovered a fine natural harbor on the adjacent New Providence island, where a fort and city (later called Nassau) sprang up. Within a few years, however, it had developed into a buccaneer base frequented by the likes of Blackbeard and Jack Rackham. Finally, pirate-turned-governor Woodes Rogers was enlisted by the British goverment to bring the colony under control in the 1720s, curtailing the privateers' raids. During the American War of Independence, the islands proved a useful source of arms for the rebels, and afterwards they welcomed fleeing loyalists who arrived with their slaves to set up plantations. Further fortunes were made from gun-running during the Civil War, and from bootleg booze during Prohibition. Since World War II, the Bahamas have experienced a tourist boom concentrated on the islands of Grand Bahama and New Providence. The billion-dollar industry employs around two-thirds of the workforce, who do not pay taxes thanks to the revenue generated by offshore finance and ships' registry fees.

GRAND BAHAMA

From a handful of sleepy fishing villages to major holiday destination within the space of 30 years, Grand Bahama, the fourth largest Bahamanian island, is one of the region's top tourist spots. More than a million visitors come every year, lured by its miles of white-sand beaches, superb diving, and duty-free shopping.

FREEPORT/LUCAYA

American entrepreneur Wallace Groves was the man behind Grand Bahama's transformation. The sprawling modern city of Freeport, together with its beach resort annex, Lucaya, is very much based on the American model. Its broad boulevards, shopping malls, and high-rise hotels are anything but Caribbean.

Garden of the Groves and Grand Bahama Museum

On the eastern outskirts of Freeport, this lush 12-acre garden was laid out in honor of Mr. and Mrs. Wallace Groves. It is landscaped with over 5,000 varieties of flowers, shrubs, and trees, and has pools fed by miniature waterfalls, meandering paths, and plenty of quiet corners. Within the grounds, the Grand Bahama Museum highlights local history with displays of Stone Age Lucayan artifacts, pirate treasure, marine life exhibits, and

Luxuriant vegetation and calm waters in Freeport's Garden of the Groves

Junkanoo costumes used in the annual Christmas to New Year Festival. *Midshipman Road. Tel: (242) 373 5668. Open: daily, 9am–4pm. Admission charge to gardens, museum free.*

JUNKANOO

Cultural highlight of the Bahamanian year, the Junkanoo carnival kicks off on Boxing Day with a "rush" (parade) through the streets of Nassau and Grand Bahama's West End. Costumed masquerades, decorated floats, dancers, and bands are urged on by drums, whistles, and home-made noisemakers in a national celebration with tangible African roots. The party atmosphere, beauty pageants, and competitions climax in the New Year's Day Parade, but visitors can get a taste of Junkanoo year-round at the Junkanoo Expo, Prince George Dock, in Nassau, New Providence.

International Bazaar

A 10-acre shopper's paradise, the architecture here could best be described as "international bizarre." It was built in 1967 as the brainchild of a Hollywood special effects set designer, and nowadays houses an international cast of boutiques and stores, which sell everything from French perfumes and Swiss watches to Japanese cameras and Irish linen. Local souvenirs are on sale in the Straw Market. *W Atlantic Drive, at W Sunrise Highway. Open: Monday to Saturday, 9am–6pm.*

Grand Bahama Tourist Office – PO Box F40251, International Bazaar, Freeport. Tel: (242) 352 8044.
Bahamas Ministry of Tourism – PO Box N3701, Nassau. Tel: (242) 322 7500.
Rawson Square Tourist Information Booth – Nassau. Tel: (242) 326 9781.

Pretty in pink: Columbus strikes a pose in front of the "Nassau-pink" Government House, Nassau

development of flashy new resort areas in Cable Beach and Paradise Island (the latter linked to Nassau by a 1,500-foot toll bridge) place New Providence firmly in the frame as a major tourist stop.

NASSAU

The busy cruise ship dock is a couple of minutes' walk from the tourist office on Rawson Square and the town center. On the west side of the square, there are horse-drawn surreys for rent. The chatty drivers provide 45-minute tours for two. Across Bay Street, Nassau's main thoroughfare and shopping district, the pink-and-white House of Assembly faces Parliament Square, (starting point for the Nassau Walk, see pages 54–5). Several attractions lie a short distance from the town center, easily reached by taxi or mopeds, which can be rented near the dock. Cheap and frequent minibus services to Cable Beach leave from Bay Street, and ferries make regular crossings to Paradise Island.

Port Lucaya

This $10-million, 6-acre site is Grand Bahama's latest shopping, dining, and entertainment complex. It overlooks a busy marina, and there are several good value cafés among the T-shirt stores and "resort wear" boutiques.

If you fancy investigating marine life in the colorful coral reefs without getting your hair wet, glass-bottomed boats make regular departures from the port. *Royal Palm Way. Open: Monday to Saturday, 9am–6pm.*

NEW PROVIDENCE

Measuring just 7 miles by 21 miles, New Providence became the chief Bahamanian island by virtue of its north coast harbor, site of present-day Nassau. This was the seat of the British administration until Independence in 1973, and there is still a rather sleepy Anglo influence in historic Nassau, with its pith-helmeted police officers, horse-drawn carriages, and shady squares. The

Ardastra Gardens and Conservation Center

Set in 5 acres of tropical gardens, the Center is home to around 300 birds and beasts, from parrots, peacocks, and iguanas, to a troupe of marching flamingos, the Bahamas's national bird. *1½ miles west of Nassau via Chippingham Road. Tel: (242) 323 5806. Open: daily, 9am–5pm. Admission charge.*

Cable Beach

The "Bahamanian Riviera," this popular and busy sand beach fronts the island's biggest and best resort hotels, such as the 1,550-room Crystal Palace Resort and

Casino. You'll find water sports galore, glass-bottomed boat trips, and fine dining opportunities.
3 miles west of Nassau via West Bay Street.

Coral World

This is a fascinating marine menagerie, displayed in tanks, pools, and aquariums spread around a waterfront site. Meet sea turtles and stingrays, and see feeding sharks and dainty starfish. The journey 20 feet below the sea in the underwater observatory is a real eye-opener.
1½ miles west at Silver Cay. Tel: (242) 328 1036. Open: daily, 9am–6pm. Admission charge. Boat transfers from downtown Nassau, Cable Beach, and Paradise Island.

Fort Charlotte

Built to guard Nassau Harbor at the end of the 18th century, this sprawling, low-slung fortress affords grand views from its hilltop site. Above the moat, the white-stone battlements are reinforced with cannons, while below ground you

can visit the dungeons.
Off West Bay Street, 1 mile west of Nassau. Tel: (242) 325 9186. Open: Monday to Saturday, 9am–4pm. Admission charge.

Paradise Island

Known as Hog Island until 1962, the developer of this small island, linked to Nassau by a toll causeway (nominal charge for pedestrians), decided a name change was necessary in order to attract tourists. There are fine beaches to the west and to the north, exclusive hotels set in manicured grounds, and the pretty Versailles Gardens and French Cloister on Paradise Island Drive, near the deluxe Ocean Club. The elegant 14th-century cloister, with its slim columns and carved capitals, was brought from the famous French pilgrimage town of Lourdes.

Marine inhabitants of the Coral World aquarium at Silver Cay

Nassau

Behind the busy port, which can handle up to ten cruise liners per day, Nassau's compact old town climbs uphill from the waterfront. It is easily explored on foot, and this relaxed walk combines a stroll down bustling Bay Street, with visits to a small selection of historic sites. *Allow 2 hours.*

Start at Parliament Square.

1 PARLIAMENT SQUARE

The traditional hub of Bahamanian government, three sides of the square are bordered by the colonial-style, pink-painted buildings of the House of Assembly, the Ministry of Finance, and the Supreme Court. In front sits an uncharacteristically young Queen Victoria flanked by cannons.
Head west along Bay Street.

2 THE STRAW MARKET

Undoubtedly a tourist trap, but fun nonetheless, the covered market is a warren of stalls piled high with every conceivable straw souvenir, from hats and bags to dolls and napkin rings.

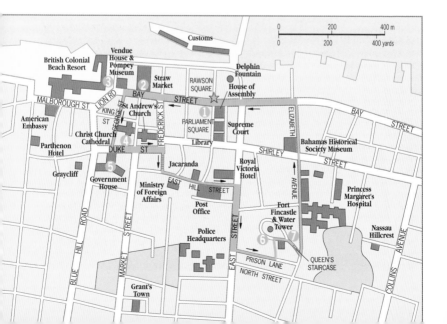

Colorful Caribbean basketwork is piled high at the Straw Market

T-shirt sellers and hair plaiters do a roaring trade, too.

3 VENDUE HOUSE AND POMPEY MUSEUM

Slave auctions were once held in this 18th-century building facing George Street. Today, the museum displays Bahamanian history exhibits and paintings by folk artist Amos Ferguson. These naive renderings of colorful local scenes are now collectors' items.
Walk up George Street to the corner of King Street.

4 CHRIST CHURCH CATHEDRAL

Built on the site of the first church in the Bahamas, the graceful interior of the 18th- to 19th-century cathedral is lined with tall windows to catch the breeze. Wall plaques bear testament to a history of fevers and shipwrecks.
Continue up George Street.

5 GOVERNMENT HOUSE

The Governor General's imposing residence sits at the top of shady George Street, clad in the official pink-and-white Bahamanian color scheme. A statue of Christopher Columbus strikes a rakish pose on the steps.
Walk east on Duke Street. Just past St. Andrew's Church, take the steps up to East Hill, site of the blue-painted Friendship sculpture, given by the people of Mexico. Turn left along East Hill Street, right on East Street, and left up Prison Lane.

6 FORT FINCASTLE AND THE WATER TOWER

Dating from 1793, the stumpy little paddle steamer-shaped fortress, with its sharp-nosed prow, never actually fired a shot in anger. It was, however, a useful lighthouse and signal station. Climb up onto the cannon-lined turret and sloping "deck" for views of the harbor. For a real panorama, take a trip up the 126-foot Water Tower.

7 QUEEN'S STAIRCASE

Take the famous sixty-six-step staircase down to Princess Margaret's Hospital and Elizabeth Avenue. The staircase was carved out of the limestone hillside by slave labor in the 18th century.
Walk down Elizabeth Avenue to rejoin Bay Street. At Shirley Street, the modest Bahamas Historical Society Museum charts local history with the aid of period maps, paintings, and photographs.

Vendue House and Pompey Museum – open: Monday to Friday, 10am–4:30pm; Saturday, 10am–1pm. Admission charge.
Fort Fincastle and the Water Tower – open: daily, dawn–dusk. Admission charge for Water Tower elevator.
Bahamas Historical Society Museum – tel: (242) 322 4231. Open: Monday to Wednesday and Friday, 10am–4pm, Saturday, 10am–noon. Free (donations).

Ship cruising is a relatively new phenomenon. Humankind has braved the Seven Seas for thousands of years in the name of exploration, war, or trade, but never as a leisure activity. Travelers generally had to work their passage, and the ocean-going part of any journey was severely uncomfortable, and frequently fraught with danger.

A list of draconian regulations, posted on board in 1849, exhorted early fare-paying passengers to "rise at 7am unless otherwise permitted by the Surgeon." Before breakfast they had "to roll up their beds, to Sweep the Decks ... and to throw the Dirt overboard."

Despite the privations encountered by pioneer cruise passengers, the concept of sea travel for pleasure caught on. By the turn of the century, cruising had arrived as a popular pastime for the idle rich, and shipping lines rose to the occasion by building opulent floating palaces. During the height of the cruising era in the 1920s and 1930s, magnificent liners, such as

Magnificent sunsets and floating swimming pools are all part of the service

CRUISING

The Caribbean's finest anchorages

the *Aquitania*, the *Normandie,* and the *Queen Mary*, set sail with several thousand passengers ensconced in the most unbelievable luxury.

Life on board was one hectic round of deck games and dancing. Guests' appetites were primed by a spot of tennis or deck quoits, before sampling menus the size of telephone directories. Packing for a cruise was a sartorial challenge. In addition to stout shoes and comfortable tweeds for pacing the deck, fashion essentials included several changes of full evening dress and mountains of jewelry. For gentlemen in search of a little shipboard romance, the 1927 cruising guide *Frantic Atlantic* reckoned a decent dinner jacket was vital: "Without it you will have no dances and no Great Moments with the young thing in crêpe-marocain on the lee of the starboard ventilator."

Though the great liners and "Golden Era" of cruising may have wasted away from the combined effects of the 1930s Depression and air travel, cruising is still the most luxurious mode of travel to this day. The romance just will not die.

Barbados

A pear-shaped island measuring 14 miles by 21 miles, Barbados lies about a hundred miles east of the Windward island chain. It was noticed, but not settled, by early Spanish and Portugese adventurers who named the island *Los Barbudos*, or "the bearded ones," after its native banyan (ficus) trees, which drop a curtain of aerial roots towards the ground. Barbados was uninhabited when the British claimed it in 1625, though its favorable climate and rich soil were to make it one of the most successful colonies in the West Indies.

The British ruled Barbados for over 300 uninterrupted years until Independence in 1966, and their influence still lingers. Familiar place names abound, from Bridgetown's Trafalgar Square to the hilly Scotland district in the northeast. The national sport (and abiding passion) is cricket, and there is even a touch of a West Country accent in the lilting Bajan speech.

There is plenty to see and do around the island; the sights are spread out around the various districts, typically named after saints. The sheltered west coast is famous for its nice hotels and seamless strip of white sand; the surf-lashed and rocky east coast is more picturesque, but swimming is dangerous.

Independence Arch on the south side of Chamberlain Bridge, Bridgetown

BRIDGETOWN

Over a third of the island's total population of 254,000 live in the capital, Bridgetown. This bustling town pivots around central Trafalgar Square, overlooked by a statue of Lord Nelson erected in 1813 (before its counterpart in London). Off the square is fast-paced Broad Street, the town's main commercial thoroughfare. To the north, part of the mellow stone Public Buildings complex is occupied by the House of Assembly. Though the site only dates from the 19th century, the Bajan parliament is the third oldest in the British Commonwealth (after Britain and Bermuda), and was founded in 1639. A short walk east, 18th-century St. Michael's Cathedral was rebuilt on the site of the original mid-17th-century church. To the south of Trafalgar Square, the Chamberlain Bridge crosses the Careenage (a finger of sea) to a handful of pleasant cafés facing the waterfront.

BARBADOS MUSEUM

Laid out in the old military prison, which formed part of the British garrison (see Garrison Savannah, opposite), this museum traces Bajan history through the ages. Collections of Amerindian artifacts, military memorabilia, and exhibits relating to sugar production and slavery are displayed in a series of old cells.

A traditional-style wooden chattel house in Barbados

There are antique maps, portraits and photographs, a children's section, and natural history displays.
St. Anne's Garrison, 1 mile south of Bridgetown. Tel: (246) 427 0201. Open: Monday to Saturday, 9am–5pm; Saturday 2–6pm. Admission charge.

GARRISON SAVANNAH

Once a British army parade ground, Garrison Savannah is now home to the Barbados Turf Club. Twenty race meetings a year take place on Saturdays on the grassy course, which is also popular with joggers. Around the Savannah, there is an interesting collection of 19th-century buildings, old barracks, and rampart ruins belonging to

---

Barbados Tourism Authority – PO Box 242, Harbour Road, Bridgetown. Tel: (246) 427 2623. There is also a pier-side information booth.

Charles Fort (built in the 17th century), and St. Anne's Fort (begun in 1704 but never completed). The distinctive red-painted Main Guard (also known as the Savannah Club) is being restored to house a reception center with information and area maps.
Off Garrison Hill (1½ miles south of Bridgetown).

ANDROMEDA GARDENS

This beautiful 6-acre garden, perched on the east coast cliffs with glimpses of the bay below, was founded in 1954. Today, it is world-renowned for its variety of exotic species – orchids, heliconia, hibiscus, palms, and cacti; and there are arches bound with fragrant stephanotis, frangipani trees, and clouds of multicolored bougainvillea. Shaded corners reveal a mass of ferns and marvelous ornamental foliage.
Bathsheba, St. Joseph District. Tel: (246) 433 9261. Open: daily, 9am–5pm. Admission charge.

BARBADOS

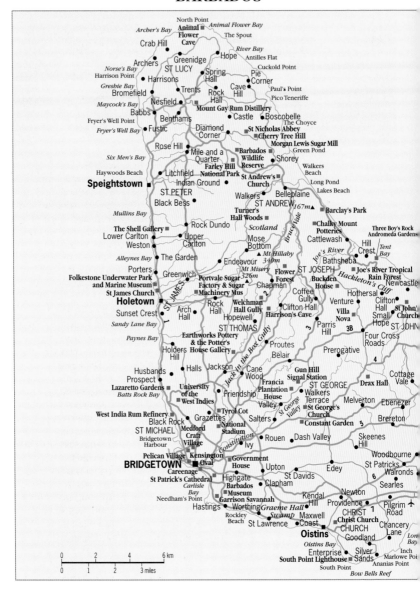

North Point
Archer's Bay Animal ■ Animal Flower Bay
Flower
Cave The Spout
Crab Hill
River Bay
Hope Antilles Flat
Archers Greenidge
Norse's Bay ST LUCY Spring Cuckold Point
Harrison Point Hall Pie
Harrisons Corner
Gresbie Bay Cave
Bromefield Trents Rock Hill Paul's Point
Maycock's Bay Nesfield Hall Pico Teneriffe
Babbs Mount Gay Rum Distillery
Benthams Castle Boscobelle
Fryer's Well Point The Choyce
Fryer's Well Bay ● Fustic Diamond St Nicholas Abbey
Corner Cherry Tree Hill
Rose Hill Morgan Lewis Sugar Mill
Mile and a Barbados ■ Green Pond
Six Men's Bay Quarter Wildlife Shorey
Farley Hill Reserve
Haywoods Beach Litchfield National Park St Andrew's Walkers
Speightstown ■ Indian Ground ● Church Beach
ST PETER Long Pond
Black Bess Walkers Belleplaine Lakes Beach
Mullins Bay ST ANDREW 167m▲ Barclay's Park
Turner's
Hall Woods
Rock Dundo Scotland ●Chalky Mount Three Boy's Rock
The Shell Gallery ■ Potteries Andromeda Gardens
Lower Carlton Upper Mose Cattlewash Hill
Weston Carlton Bottom Crest Tent
Alleynes Bay ● The Garden Bay
Endeavour ▲ Mt Hillaby Bathsheba
Porters 340m
Folkestone Underwater Park Greenwich ▲Mt Misery Flower ST JOSEPH ●Joe's River Tropical
and Marine Museum Portvale Sugar 326m Forest Rain Forest
St James Church Factory & Sugar Chapman Buckden Newcastle
Holetown ■ Machinery Mus House Hothersal
Sunset Crest ● Rock Welchman Coffee Clifton
Arch Hall Hall Gully Gully Hall St John's
Sandy Lane Bay Hall Hopewell Clifton Hall Venture Church
Harrison's Cave Villa Small Hope ST JOHN
Paynes Bay ST THOMAS Nova Hope
Earthworks Pottery Parris 3B
& the Potter's Hill Four Cross
Holders House Gallery Proutes Prerogative Roads
Hill Belair 4
Husbands Halls Jackson Cane
Prospect Wood Gun Hill Cottage
Lazaretto Gardens ● University Francia Signal Station Drax Hall Vale
Batts Rock Bay of the Plantation ST GEORGE
West Indies Friendship House Walkers Melverton Ebenezer
West India Rum Refinery ■ Terrace St George's Brereton
Black Rock Tyrol Cot Valley Church
ST MICHAEL Grazettes National Salters Constant Garden 5 Skeenes
Medford Stadium Hill
Bridgetown Craft Rouen Dash Valley Woodbourne
Harbour Village Ivy St Patricks
Pelican Village ● Government Edey Walronds
BRIDGETOWN ■ Kensington House Upton 6
Oval Highgate St Davids Searles
Careenage Clapham
St Patrick's Cathedral Barbados Newton
Carlisle Museum Kendal Providence ● Pilgrim
Bay Garrison Savannah Hill CHRIST Road
Needham's Point Hastings Worthing Graeme Hall Maxwell Christ Church Chancery
Rockley Swamp Coast CHURCH Lane
Beach St Lawrence Oistins ■ Goodland
Oistins Bay Lon
Enterprise ● Silver Inch
South Point Lighthouse ● Sands Marlowe Poi
South Point Ananias Point
Bow Bells Reef

Joe's River
Bruce Vale
Hackleton's Cliff
ST JAMES
Jack in the Box Gully
St George Valley
Constitution

0   2   4   6 km
0   1   2   3 miles

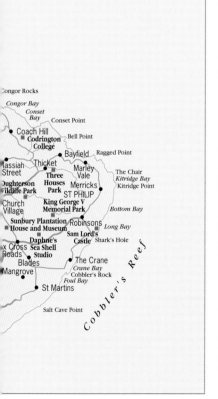

ANIMAL FLOWER CAVE

Twenty-seven deep steps lead down to this underground cave in the cliffs. Paddle about through the stalactites and stalagmites with a guide and watch yellow, orange, and green sea anenomes wave their tiny tentacles in the rock pools. There is also a swimming hole.

St. Lucy District. Tel: (246) 439 8797.
Open: daily, 9am–5pm. Admission charge.

BARBADOS WILDLIFE RESERVE

Set in 4 acres of natural mahogany forest, the reserve provides a safe haven for green monkeys, or vervets, considered a pest by local farmers. Brick paths through the woods offer a chance to spot Brocket deer, lumbering tortoises, porcupines, agoutis, and playful otters. There is also a walk-through aviary, reptile cages, and a cayman pool, where these alligator-like creatures bask on the sunny banks. The Grenade Hall Signal Station by the parking lot was first used to keep an eye on the slaves in the cane fields, and then for spotting approaching ships. Pleasantly shaded, well-marked nature trails in the adjacent Grenade Hall Forest provide an introduction to the local flora.

St. Peter District. Tel: (246) 422 8826.
Open: daily, 10am–5pm. Admission charge.

The elegant Francia Plantation house is decorated with antique Barbadian furniture

CODRINGTON COLLEGE

A magnificent driveway lined with lofty cabbage palms leads down to the elegant façade of this Anglican theological college. It was founded in 1745, and named after its benefactor, Christopher Codrington, a Governor of the Leeward Islands who was brought up in the original Codrington mansion, now the Principal's Lodge. The attractive grounds are open to view, with lily ponds and a woodland trail.

St. John District. Tel: (246) 433 1274. Open: daily, 10am–4pm. Admission charge.

FARLEY HILL NATIONAL PARK

A good spot to relax with a picnic, this national park is perched on a 900-foot cliff with views over the rugged Scotland district. Laid out around the ruins of a 19th-century plantation house, the lovely landscaped grounds are planted with a wide variety of trees.

St. Peter District. Tel: (246) 422 3555. Open: daily, 8:30am–6pm. Admission charge for vehicles.

MORGAN LEWIS SUGAR MILL

This 250-year-old sugar-grinding mill is the largest surviving windmill in the Caribbean region, complete with restored machinery and sails. It was working right up until 1944, and affords panoramic views over the surrounding countryside.

St. Andrew District. Tel: (246) 422 9222. Open: Monday to Friday, 9am–5pm. Admission charge.

Three hundred years ago about 500 cane-crushing windmills existed in Barbados

ST. NICHOLAS ABBEY

A gabled manor house built around 1650 to 1660, the "abbey" is a rare example of Jacobean architecture in the Caribbean. The ground floor is lined with panelled walls (an old trick for concealing damp blisters in the tropics) and has been carefully restored. Furnishings include an ingenious multipurpose "gentleman's chair" that could cover all eventualities, from toilet to reading stand. Walk around the gardens and look in the bathhouse, equipped with a variety of hip baths.

St. Peter District. Tel: (246) 422 8725. Open: Monday to Friday, 10am–3pm. Admission charge.

SUNBURY PLANTATION HOUSE

This comfortable 300-year-old plantation house first appeared on a map dated 1681 and was a family home until 1985. It has survived several major hurricanes thanks to its sturdy 2½-foot thick walls.

HISTORIC HOMES

In addition to St. Nicholas Abbey and the Sunbury Plantation House, Barbados has two notable historic homes.

Tyrol Cot, just north of Bridgetown, was home to former premier, Sir Grantley Adams. Today it is the centerpiece of Barbados's first architectural heritage museum. *(Tel: (246) 424 2074. Open: Monday to Friday, 9am–5pm. Admission charge.)* The elegant turn-of-the-century **Francia Plantation** is a working vegetable plantation with terraced gardens overlooking the St. George Valley. *(Tel: (809) 429 0474. Open: Monday to Friday, 10am–4pm. Admission charge.)*

Fresh flowers and potted plants add a homely air to the reception rooms, which contain mahogany furniture, antique silver and glassware, tall hurricane lamps, and 19th-century engravings. Upstairs, there are displays of Victorian clothing laid out on four-poster beds. An old yam cellar houses agricultural artifacts, domestic utensils, and a cart and carriage museum; several historic conveyances are on display in the gardens. Refreshments are also available here.

St. Philip District. Tel: (246) 423 6270. Open: daily, 10am–4:30pm. Admission charge.

The unusual gabled façade of 17th-century St. Nicholas Abbey

WELCHMAN HALL GULLY

A favorite with plant lovers, this lush wooded gully was first laid out as a botanical walk in the 1860s. Abandoned for many years, it was rescued by the Barbados National Trust in 1962, and restored to a cool forest habitat with a mile-long path, edged by towering bamboo, palms, nutmeg, clove, and fig trees. Families of green monkeys crash about overhead in the late afternoon.

St. Joseph District. Tel: (246) 438 6671. Open: daily, 9am–5pm. Admission charge.

Bermuda

*T*he Bermuda Islands, Britain's oldest colony, and spiritual home of the ubiquitous knee-length Bermuda shorts, first introduced by the British military around the turn of the century, lie about 650 miles east of Cape Hatteras, North Carolina, in the Atlantic Ocean. Warmed by the Gulf Stream and protected by the world's most northerly coral reefs, seven of the 150 islands are connected by bridges and causeways to form Bermuda, which has three cruise ship docks: Hamilton (the capital), St. George, and the Royal Naval Dockyard in the West End.

The islands were discovered by Spanish explorer Juan Bermudez in 1503, but not settled until the early 17th century, by the British after Sir George Somers' was shipwrecked off St. George's Island in 1609. Today, Bermuda is a popular summer season destination, decidedly British with pubs and cricket pitches, luxuriant gardens and pretty pastel-painted cottages. It is also usually the only port of call that allows passengers a full three or four days for exploring.

HAMILTON

Bermuda's main cruise port and capital, Hamilton is a top shopping spot and an excellent base for trips around the island. The cruise ship berths are a minute's walk from bustling Front Street. When you want to take a break from shopping, there are several attractions to visit. On Church Street is the 19th-century Bermuda Cathedral. Close by, on the same street, Bermuda National Gallery's collections of 15th- to 19th-century oil

BERMUDA

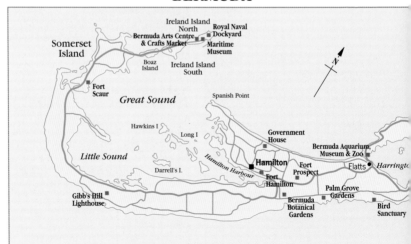

paintings and watercolors are housed in the modern City Hall. On Parliament Street, off Front Street, you can also visit on weekdays the Sessions House (or Supreme Court), seat of the second oldest parliament in the world. A short walk west of Front Street brings you to Par-la-Ville Gardens and the Perot Post Office on Queen Street. Here you will find the Historical Society Museum with its eclectic collection of antiques and colonial memorabilia.

City Hall – open: Monday to Friday, 9am–5pm. Admission charge. Historical Society Museum – open: Monday to Saturday, 9:30am–3:30pm. Free.

Bermuda Department of Tourism – Global House, 43 Church Street, Hamilton HM12.
Visitors Service Bureau – Front Street, Hamilton. Tel: (441) 292 0023.

FORT HAMILTON
East of the city center, Fort Hamilton, complete with moat, affords a panoramic view of the town and harbor. The Bermuda Island Pipe Band performs the Skirling Ceremony here, a distinctly Scottish affair complete with kilts, drums, dancers, and bagpipes (check with the Visitors Service Bureau for details).

Off Happy Valley Road. Open: daily, 9:30am–5pm. Free.

THE BERMUDA TRIANGLE
A triangular patch of the Atlantic Ocean bounded by Bermuda, Florida, and Puerto Rico, the "Bermuda Triangle" is the legendary graveyard for dozens of boats and planes lost without trace in this corner of the world. Some say accident, while others claim the area exerts a powerful and potentially lethal force. Whatever the cause, at least 100 ships and 1,000 sailors have disappeared in the region during the latter part of this century. One of the strangest incidents was the disappearance of five U.S. torpedo bombers that took off on a routine two-hour patrol from Fort Lauderdale on December 5, 1944. Just before they were due to return, the patrol leader was asked to describe his position and replied, "We don't know which way west is. Everything is wrong . . . even the ocean doesn't look as it should." After radio contact was lost, a search plane went out – it also disappeared. The U.S. Navy commenced a five-year study, Project Magnet, to investigate the possibility of magnetic interference, but nothing was ever proved.

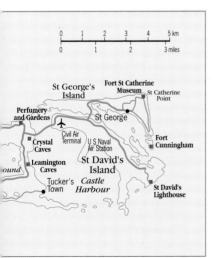

In the 18th and 19th centuries, sailors donated plants to the Botanical Gardens

BERMUDA AQUARIUM, MUSEUM, AND ZOO

The Bermuda Aquarium offers a fascinating insight into the subtropical and tropical marine world. You'll find an amazing collection of brilliantly colored sea creatures, from tiny fish and sea horses to hefty Galapagos turtles, plus a natural history museum and a Zoological Garden with a screeching, dazzling, entertaining collection of tropical birds and animals.

North Shore Road, Harrington Sound. Tel: (441) 293 2727. Open: daily, 9am–5pm. Admission charge.

BERMUDA BOTANICAL GARDENS ("CAMDEN")

Camden, the Bermuda premier's official residence, is set in these 36-acre botanical gardens founded in 1898. As well as formal gardens and an aromatic garden for visually-impaired visitors, there are subtropical fruit groves, rare Bermuda cedars, banyan trees, an orchid house, and an aviary.

Berry Hill Road, Paget (east of Hamilton). Tel: (441) 236 5732. Open: Tuesday (unless official functions are scheduled), Wednesday, and Friday, noon–2pm. Free.

CRYSTAL CAVES

Nature is at its most bizarre in these subterranean caves. Fantastic arrangements of stalactites and stalagmites create an eerie landscape around underground saltwater lagoons. Pontoon bridges edge around the pools, which reach depths of 55 feet, though the water is so crystal clear you'd think the bottom was just inches away.

Wilkinson Avenue, off Harrington Sound Road, Baileys Bay. Tel: (441) 293 0640. Open: April to October, daily, 9:30am–4:30pm; check winter schedules. Admission charge.

FORT ST. CATHERINE MUSEUM

Fort St. Catherine was founded in 1614 on the northeastern tip of the islands, where the survivors of Sir George Somers' shipwreck supposedly first set foot on Bermuda (see page 64). It was constantly refortified against the threat of invasion (which never came), and has battlements 25 feet thick, plus powerful 18-ton muzzle-loading cannons. Inside, there are excellent historical displays, an audio-visual tour of the islands' military outposts, a re-created cookhouse, and replicas of the British Crown Jewels.

Barry Road, St. George. Tel: (441) 297 1920. Open: daily, 10am–4:30pm. Admission charge.

ROYAL NAVAL DOCKYARD

The naval dockyard was developed in the 19th century, inspired by the Duke of Wellington's vision that Bermuda should become the "Gibraltar of the West." Heavily fortified and equipped with numerous ordnance buildings, barracks, and a cooperage, the yard also boasts a

Today, cruise passengers come to shop at Bermuda's Royal Naval Dockyard

splendid 100-foot-high clocktower and the world's largest floating dry dock. The dockyard's new role is as a shopping, sightseeing, dining, and nightlife complex.

Bermuda Arts Centre and Craft Market

The Arts Centre occupies the former cooperage building, providing a display area for contemporary arts and crafts and exhibitions by local artists and traveling shows. You can watch local craftspeople at work in the Bermuda Clayworks Pottery and at the Craft Market where artisans produce and sell souvenirs, such as handblown glass, quilts, wood carvings, and traditional folkloric dolls.
Arts Center. Tel: (441) 234 2809. Open: daily, 10am–5pm. Craft Market. Tel: (441) 234 3208. Open: daily, 9.30am–5pm. Free.

Maritime Museum

Housed in the old Powder Magazine, this interesting and informative museum illustrates Bermuda's long and colorful maritime history, from whaling and shipbuilding to piracy and rum-running. There are intricate model ships and nautical knick-knacks; gold and artifacts salvaged from wrecks are displayed in the well-stocked Treasure House. There is also an Age of Discovery exhibit.
Tel: (441) 234 1418. Open: daily, 9:30am–4:30pm May to November, 10am–4:30pm December to April. Admission charge.

Location: Royal Naval Dockyard is 15 miles northwest of Hamilton. Ferries (30-minute journey time) depart from Hamilton, and there are good bus services.

St. George

This picturesque port was the original capital of Bermuda (transferred to Hamilton in 1815), and has been immaculately preserved. *Allow 2–3 hours.*

1 DELIVERANCE

Near the pier on Ordnance Island, this tub-like vessel is a faithful replica of the 17th-century ship *Deliverance*; one of two sailing ships built by Sir George Somers's crew (see page 64) in order to continue their journey to America.
Cross the bridge to King's Square and look right.

2 TOWN HALL

A splendid colonial building dating from 1782, the Town Hall is home to the Bermuda Journey multimedia presentation. This is a good opportunity to catch up on Bermudan history, and an introduction in what to see and do around the island.
From the top right-hand corner of the square, head east on King Street.

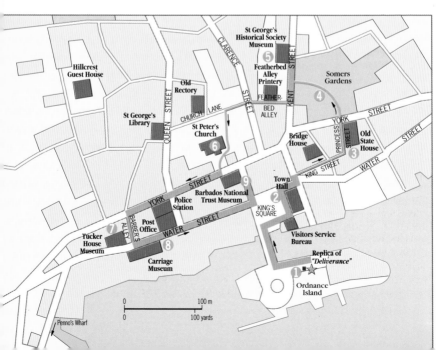

3 OLD STATE HOUSE

The Old State House was built in the Italian fashion by Governor Nathaniel Butler – who believed Bermuda was on the same latitude as Italy.
Walk north on Princess Street.

4 SOMERS GARDENS

Buried here is the heart of Sir George Somers, who bravely sailed back to Bermuda from Jamestown, Virginia, to find supplies for the beleaguered colonists.
Cross Kent Street to Featherbed Alley.

5 ST. GEORGE'S HISTORICAL SOCIETY MUSEUM AND FEATHERBED ALLEY PRINTERY

The Historical Museum, housed in a typical 18th-century Bermudan cottage, depicts bygone island life. Just around the corner, the Printery contains an antique press.
Head west across Clarence Street onto Church Lane.

6 ST. PETER'S CHURCH

The churchyard is fascinating in itself. Take a good look round the gravestones (some are over 300 years old) before entering the church, built in 1713. The church treasure is displayed in the vestry.
Exit right onto York Street, cross Queen Street, turn left into Barber's Alley, and turn right onto Water Street.

7 TUCKER HOUSE MUSEUM

Once home to one of Bermuda's most important families (various Tuckers were governors, bishops, and one even made it to Treasurer of the United States), this fine historic house is furnished with collections of cedar furniture, oil paintings, silver, and antiques.
Cross Water Street.

Deliverance – open: daily, 9am–6pm; April to November, reduced hours in winter. Admission charge.
Town Hall – open: Monday to Saturday, 10am–4pm. Free.
Old State House – open: most Wednesdays, 10am–4pm. Free.
St. George's Historical Society Museum – open: Monday to Friday, 10am–4pm. Joint admission charge with printery below.
Featherbed Alley Printery – open: Monday to Friday, 10am–4pm. Joint admission with Historical Society Museum (above).
Tucker House Museum – open: Monday to Saturday, 10am–4pm. Admission charge.
Carriage Museum – open: Monday to Friday, 10am–4pm. Admission by donation.
Bermuda National Trust Museum – open: Monday to Saturday, 10am–4pm; Sunday, 1–4pm. Admission charge.

8 CARRIAGE MUSEUM

The first automobiles didn't arrive in Bermuda until 1946, so until then Bermudans got around in a variety of horse-drawn carriages.
Head east on Water Street to King's Square.

9 BERMUDA NATIONAL TRUST MUSEUM

Island history exhibits include an interesting section on Bermuda's role in the American Civil War. The island was a vital staging post for Confederate blockade runners involved in forwarding arms from Europe to the Confederacy.

Cayman Islands

A group of three islands 150 miles south of Cuba, the Caymans are famous for banking, diving, and tax-free shopping. These low coral islands are in fact the summits of underwater mountains and were spotted by Christopher Columbus on his fourth voyage in 1503. He named them *Las Tortugas*, "the turtles," for their once-abundant turtle population. The name did not stick, however, and the islands were rechristened the *Caymanas* after the Carib Indian word for crocodiles, which may have once lived here.

Swimming with friendly stingrays off the shores of Grand Cayman

Caymanians. The rest live on the little sister islands of Cayman Brac and Little Cayman to the northeast.

GRAND CAYMAN

An ever-popular stop with the cruising fraternity, Grand Cayman is relaxed, well-organized, and virtually crime-free. It is easy to get around, with local buses as well as taxis plying the northbound road from George Town past the alluring white-sand expanse of Seven Mile Beach to West Bay, covering the island's main attractions along the way.

GEORGE TOWN

As you step ashore at George Town, the tourist information booth offers helpful information and maps, including a Historic Walking Tour of the town. The main shopping areas are around Fort Street and the Kirk Freeport Plaza.

The islands were ceded to Britain (together with Jamaica) in the Treaty of Madrid (1670), and were governed in tandem with the larger island. When Jamaica claimed independence in 1961, the Caymans chose to become a British Crown Colony.

The largest and southernmost island of the group is Grand Cayman, home to around 26,000 of the 28,000

GRAND CAYMAN

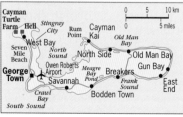

Atlantis Submarine

Nondivers should grab this opportunity to experience the amazing Cayman Wall from the comfort of their own porthole. The colorful world of corals and sponges is inhabited by a breathtaking parade of weird and wonderful marine life (see pages 72–3).

*George Town Harbor. Tel: (345) 949
7700. Open: Monday to Saturday,
9am–3pm. Admission charge.*

Cayman Islands National Museum

Spruced up and freshly painted, the Old
Courthouse and Jail now houses a fine
range of exhibits charting the island's
turbulent history of pirates and wreckers,
and displays of shipbuilding, rope-
making, and turtle-hunting.
*South Church Street, at Shedden Road. Tel:
(345) 949 8368. Open: Monday to Friday,
9:30am–5:30pm; Saturday, 10am–4pm.
Admission charge.*

Cayman Turtle Farm

This is the world's only commercial
green turtle farm. It plays a conservation
role by releasing a small percentage of its
captive-bred turtles back into the wild.
Here you'll find thousands of turtles in
varying stages of development, from
incubating eggs to 600-pound monsters.
Cold-hearted visitors can sample
traditional Cayman turtle dishes in the
café. (NB. Turtle products cannot be
imported into the U.S. or U.K.)
*West Bay Road. Tel: (345) 949 3894.
Open: daily, 9am–5pm. Admission charge.*

HELL

A well-trodden path, the road to Hell
ends up in a touristy spread of gift shops
and T-shirt sellers. The weathered
outcrop of iron-stone you've come to see
is over 1½ million years old. Send a
postcard – and get the Hell out!
West Bay Road, West Bay.

STINGRAY CITY

Touted as "the best 12-foot dive in the
world," this extraordinary dive and
snorkel site brings its many visitors
within petting distance of friendly

stingrays, some of which measure six feet
from wingtip to wingtip. If entering the
water sounds a little too thrilling, boats
allow passengers to at least watch the
graceful creatures in the gin-clear sea.
North Sound.

**Cayman Islands Department of
Tourism** – The Pavilion Cricket
Square, George Town, Grand
Cayman. Tel: (345) 949 0623.

Caymanians have adopted the sea turtle
as their national symbol

UNDERWATER WORLD

"Ah, but you should be here at Carnival time," they say. See the brilliant colors, the swirling costumes, the pretty people, and the vaguely sinister folkloric figures that lend such an exotic air to the Caribbean scene. Well, it

is Carnival time every day of the year, just a few feet (or even inches) below the surface of the glassy azure sea. The Caribbean region offers some of the most magnificent underwater scenery in the world, and it is yours for the price of a snorkel. In fact, you don't even have to get your feet wet, as flotillas of glass-bottomed boats and minisubmarines ferry visitors out over the reefs to view the colorful spectacle below.

Coral reefs are living entities built by limestone-secreting polyps. The forests of staghorn and elkhorn corals, delicate sea fans, feathers, and whips of soft coral provide a fantastic backdrop for all manner of cute and bizarre sea creatures. Darting electric blue kissing fish (chromis), rock beauties, elegant grey angel fish, and busy shoals of their black-and-yellow striped cousins, the sergeant majors, patrol beneath the waves. Sharp-beaked parrot fish crunch thoughtfully on chunks of hard coral, extracting the polyps and algae, while elusive eels lurk in crevices, their searching eyes also on the look-out for lunch. Decorator crabs – so called for their habit of adorning their shells with an eclectic array of camouflage materials – scramble around the rocks surrounded by starfish, sea urchins, and lobsters

Top dive spots in the Caribbean

include Bonaire and Curaçao (with a 12-acre underwater park), both in the Dutch Antilles; reef and wreck sites are in the Virgin Islands, the Bahamas, Antigua, Barbados, and the French island of Martinique. Probably the most spectacular diving of all is in the Cayman Islands, where the famous Cayman Wall plummets 20,000 feet straight down to the sea bed. Grand Cayman's other claim to fame is "Stingray City" in the sheltered waters of the North Sound, where divers and snorkelers can experience close encounters with huge semitame stingrays.

Petrified forests of delicate coral, inquisitive sharks, shy turtles, and brilliant queen angelfish are all part of the scenery beneath the waves

Dominica

*T*he "Nature Island of the Caribbean," Dominica (pronounced *Dom-in-eeker*) is lush, green, mountainous, and, almost invariably, wet. The Carib Indians called it *Wai'tukubuli*, meaning "tall is her body," and Dominica's soaring interior towers up to a peak of 4,500 feet from a base that measures just 29 miles by 16 miles.

They say that of all the Caribbean islands, Christopher Columbus would have least trouble recognizing Dominica today, as it has changed so little. He landed here on November 3, 1493, a Sunday; hence its name. The warlike Carib inhabitants discouraged early European settlers, and the wild jungle interior became a sanctuary for runaway slaves, and for Caribs flushed from other islands by the colonists.

Despite a controlling British influence from 1763 until independence in 1978, Dominica retains few reminders of its former colonial masters. English may be the island's official language, but most of the locals speak French *patois*.

Roseau market

It has always been hard to make a living on Dominica, so the island has remained largely undeveloped. This has aided the survival of the last remaining Carib people, once widespread throughout the Caribbean, and is also a trump card in courting the ecotourism market.

ROSEAU

The island capital, Roseau reaches south of the Roseau River mouth in a grid of busy streets lined with weather-beaten wooden buildings. Sagging balconies, peeling gingerbread, and rusty tin roofs give it a rather tired and fading air, but there is plenty of life in the open-air market by the river. Set back from the waterfront, off King George V Street, the old cobbled market, Dawbiney Place, has been restored with a couple of tree-shaded benches and a tourist office booth beneath a cast-iron canopy.

The 19th-century stone Cathedral of the Assumption, reached via Church Street, sits on a small hill next to the manse. One of the island's best hotels occupies the remains of 18th-century Fort Young, once the town's main defense. Cruise passengers arriving at the Bayfront terminal in Roseau will find it a handy starting point for expeditions up into the Roseau Valley and into Morne Trois Pitons National Park in the central highlands.

Botanical Gardens

Within walking distance of the waterfront, this 40-acre site nestles in the lee of Morne (Mount) Bruce, on the edge of town. The gardens were established in 1890 on the site of a former sugar plantation. Today, the spreading lawns are a popular recreation area, with over 150 different plants and trees, including a

DOMINICA

Dominica Passage

giant baobab tree (Dominica's national tree) pinning a school bus to the ground exactly where it fell during Hurricane David in 1979. An aviary houses examples of both of Dominica's indigenous and now endangered parrots: the purple-breasted Sisserou (or Imperial) and smaller red-necked Jaco parrot.

East of the town center. Open: daily, 6am–dusk. Free.

> **Dominica Division of Tourism** – PO Box 293, Roseau. Tel: (767) 448 2351. Also information booths at Dawbiney Place and Cabrits National Park.

Traces of iron-color rocks and boulders around the Trafalgar Falls

Trafalgar Falls

Trafalgar Falls is a popular side trip from the capital. Minibuses trundle to within a 10-minute walk of these beautiful 200-foot falls. From the parking lot, there is a steep clamber up to the observation point, and sensible shoes are a must. The twin falls cascade down either side of a towering green-cloaked cliff face, bounce on the riverbed boulders, and cool the air with their spray. Guides lead expeditions up to a second vantage point or down to the river, which is strewn with black and orange rocks – dyed by traces of iron in the water.

Roseau Valley (east of town). Free; charge for guides.

CARIB TERRITORY

This 3,700-acre territory on the Atlantic coast of the island was given to descendants of the Carib people in 1903. Around 3,000 Caribs live here, though most are mixed-race these days, and they have abandoned their simple thatched huts (*carbets*) in favor of wooden houses. Agriculture and fishing are the main occupations, and the Caribs still practice traditional skills of canoe-making and basket-weaving. Mats, hats, baskets, and bags are on sale throughout the island. A favorite souvenir item is the "wife-leader," a cone of loosely woven straw that fastens on to a finger when pulled tight.
South of Marigot.

MORNE TROIS PITONS NATIONAL PARK

This 17,000-acre national park encompasses a great tract of primordial rain forest, mountains, lakes, and sulphur springs. To reach many of the sights, such as the seething, volcanic Boiling Lake and sulphurous fumaroles (volcanic vents) of the Valley of Desolation, a serious full-day hike is required.

However, a new road into the park from Laudat gives access to Freshwater Lake (at 2,500 feet above sea level), and it is a pleasant two-hour round trip up to beautiful Boeri Lake. Alternatively, you could make tracks for the spectacular Middleham Falls. Island tours usually take in Emerald Pool, on the east side of the park. A 10-minute walk from the roadside through the forest ends up at a pretty water grotto, which is topped by a tiny waterfall.

PORTSMOUTH AND THE NORTHWEST

Although Portsmouth is Dominica's second largest town, it's dusty, sleepy, and, with the exception of a couple of hopeful T-shirt sellers, apparently quite unaffected by the activity of the small modern Cabrits Cruise Ship berth nearby. The town overlooks the thin black sand beaches and clear blue waters of wide, sheltered Prince Rupert Bay. Drake and Hawkins would stop off here to trade with the Caribs and resupply their ships, and the site was chosen for Dominica's first capital, which was later moved to Roseau.

Passengers disembarking here will find themselves immediately in the Cabrits National Park, where tour buses and taxi drivers are available. The park is the only attraction in the immediate vicinity, though there is a picturesque cluster of brightly painted wooden rowboats for rent at the mouth of Indian River to the south of town. Farther afield, there are tour bus excursions to the Northern Forest Reserve on the slopes of Morne Diablotin, with an opportunity to spot Dominica's rare Sisserou and Jaco parrots.

CABRITS NATIONAL PARK

On the north shore of Prince Rupert Bay, the national park incorporates the scattered remnants of Fort Shirley and assorted military outposts dating from 1765. The ruins of the 18th-century fort afford tremendous views across the bay, and there are various partially restored stone buildings dotted about the hillside lawns, including the Powder Magazine, which houses a small museum. Marked trails scramble up slippery, thickly wooded slopes to the crumbling Commandant's Quarters, and other buildings swallowed up by the forest. *Open: daily, 8am–4pm. Free.*

Fisher at Scotts Head village on Dominica's southwest coast

Grenada

*T*he "Spice Isle of the Caribbean" lies at the southernmost tip of the Grenadines, and is one of the world's chief producers of nutmeg, plus large quantities of mace (a by-product of the nutmeg tree), cloves, cinnamon, and ginger. Here, you can literally smell spices on the breeze.

Just 21 miles by 12 miles, Grenada packs an astonishing variety of natural beauty into a relatively small area. It is ringed by superb white-sand beaches, while the mountainous interior climbs steeply past spice plantations, rain forests, gentle streams, and cascading waterfalls to the island's highest point of Mt. St. Catherine (2,757 feet/838m).

Columbus sighted the island on his third voyage in 1498. He named it *Concepción*, but future generations of Spanish sailors likened it to the hills of their native Grenada. The name stuck, albeit with a change of accent (it's pronounced *Gra-nay-da*) after a century of French occupation from 1650 onwards.

After years of fighting, the British

finally gained control of Grenada in 1783, and kept it until independence in 1974. Grenada hit the world headlines in 1983, when a joint U.S.-Eastern Caribbean rescue mission restored peace on the island after the leftist leader Maurice Bishop was deposed and subsequently executed in an uprising by members of his own party. Since then, things have returned to normal.

The island's tourist industry is one of the most carefully regulated in the region, with strict rules designed to preserve the enviroment. No building can stand taller than a palm tree or be constructed less than 165 feet back from the highwater mark.

ST. GEORGE'S

Long regarded as the prettiest harbor in the Caribbean, St. George's is backed by a tight circle of hills, formed by an extinct volcanic crater. The mouth of the harbor is guarded by the French-built Fort George. Behind the warehouses of the horseshoe-shaped Carenage (inner harbor), pastel-painted buildings cling to the hillside like limpets lining the precipitous streets.

The waterfront Carenage in Grenada's capital, St. George's

GRENADA & CARRIACOU

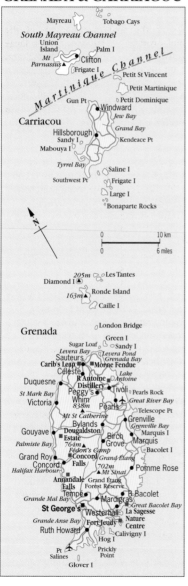

A colorful bird's-eye view of St. George's Market Square

There's a helpful tourist office right on the pier, with a supply of free island maps and walking tour guides to the town. The center of St. George's is located west of the harbor, across the hill. You can reach it via the Sendall Tunnel, which connects with the seafront Esplanade. If you visit on a Saturday, don't miss the brilliant spice and produce market on Market Square. It is one of the most colorful and photogenic in the whole Caribbean.

Grenada National Museum

This small museum is housed in an old French army barracks (built 1704), on the west side of the Carenage. It covers local history and culture from the earliest cannibal Caribs to the present day, including ancient artifacts, colonial knick-knacks, and a look at events leading up to the "friendly invasion" of 1983. *Monckton Street off Young Street. Tel: (473) 440 3725. Open: Monday to Friday, 9am–4:30pm; Saturday, 10am–1pm. Admission charge.*

Grenada Tourism Department – PO Box 293, The Carenage, St. George's. Tel: (473) 440 2001.

Brightly painted boats drawn up on the sands of Grand Anse Beach

CONCORD FALLS

There are three waterfalls here in the Concord Valley. The lowest is accessible by a winding road from the coast, and is a popular spot on any tour of the island. You can swim in the natural pool for a nominal fee. It is a 25-minute hike up to the second fall, and another hour-plus to the 65-foot-tall top fall.

7 miles northwest of St. George's.

DOUGALDSTON ESTATE

Most of the island's spices are grown on this 800-acre spice plantation, and although it has fallen on hard times, it still makes a fascinating visit. Tours of the old wooden "factory" include an introduction to a wide variety of spices, from cinnamon and cloves to tonka beans (a vanilla substitute) and allspice. All the while, a local guide explains the old-style processing methods. Mixed bags of spices only cost a couple of dollars and make a great potpourri.

Near Gouyave. Open: Monday to Friday, 9am–4pm, Saturday, 10am–1pm. Free.

GOUYAVE

Though *gouyave* actually means "guava" in French, this little clapboard town is the nutmeg capital of Grenada. Nutmeg was introduced to the island by British planters returning home from the East Indies in the 1830s. As one of the world's top nutmeg producers, Grenada even features the nutmeg on its national flag. Take a tour around the Grenada Nutmeg Cooperative for the lowdown on this spice and its waxy by-product, mace. Afterwards, wander down to the beach for a view of the colorful fishing boats drawn up on the sand.

9 miles north of St. George's. Grenada Nutmeg Cooperative – open: Monday to

Saturday, 9am–4pm. Free, but tip the guide a dollar or two.

GRANDE ANSE BAY

This is the best beach on the island for day trippers. It comprises 2 miles of gleaming white sands, with water sports, shopping, and dining facilities.
3 miles south of St. George's.

GRAND ÉTANG AND ANNANDALE FALLS

High in the Central Mountain Range, the 30-acre Grand Étang crater lake nestles in the forest, a cool 1,740 feet above sea level. There are forest trails and walks around the lake – it takes about an hour to go all the way around. Keep an eye out for the mona monkeys introduced from West Africa over 350 years ago, and check out the exhibits in the roadside Information Centre.

Closer to St. George's, the Annandale Falls and Visitor's Center is another favorite stop along the road. The 30-foot-high waterfall splashes down into a bathing pool, bordered by an herb and spice garden. Park guides give narrated walks, plus there is swimming, refreshments, crafts, and spice stalls.
7 miles northwest of St. George's in the Grand Étang Forest Reserve. Tel: (473) 440 2452. Open: daily, 9am–4pm. Admission charge.
Grand Étang Information Center – open: Monday to Saturday, 8am–4pm, and Sundays when cruise ships are in. Visitor Center – open: daily, 8am–5pm.

CARIB'S LEAP/LEAPER'S HILL

The 100-foot-high Carib's Leap cliff rears straight up from the sea. In 1651,

CARRIACOU

An occasional stop for smaller cruise ships, the diminutive island of Carriacou (8 miles by 5 miles) is famed for its smuggling, its schooners, and the locals' tolerance for Trinidadian *Jack Iron*, a spirit so eye-swivellingly strong (160 percent proof) that it causes ice to sink. Hillsborough is the main settlement, with a bustling waterfront where you can see the graceful local-built cedar schooners and a Historical Museum in a restored cotton ginnery (mill) on Paterson Street. The beaches are gorgeous, but don't overdo the *Jack Iron*, or you may miss your boat!

the last of the island's Carib Indians preferred to jump off here and thus commit suicide rather than surrender to French colonists. This tragic event is also recalled in the name of the nearby settlement of Sauteurs (in French, "the leapers").
20 miles north of St. George's.

Swimming is allowed in the freshwater pool fed by the Annandale Falls

PIRATES OF THE

The dastardly likes of Henry Morgan, Edward Teach (Blackbeard), "Calico Jack" Rackham (so called for his predilection for striped pants), and their cut-throat, rum-swigging, peg-legged cronies really did exist. And they caused havoc around the Caribbean region during the 16th and 17th centuries.

The region's early "sailors of fortune" were known as *boucaniers*, or buccaneers, a name derived from French hunter-adventurers who made a living from supplying passing ships with dried meat cured in smokehouses called *boucanes*. Ambitious buccaneers soon abandoned the food-service trade to pursue richer pickings in the form of Spanish galleons. Laden with gold and precious gems from the New World, these floating treasure houses made tempting targets, and many buccaneers made the transition to a life of piracy, via a spell as an officially sanctioned privateer. Armed with a

government license, or Letter of Marque, privateers were authorized to capture enemy ships in times of war. Once hostilities ceased, however, few felt inclined to resume a law-abiding lifestyle, and the buccaneer-privateers

Tales of buried treasure and dastardly pirates abound in Caribbean folklore

(also called freebooters or filibusters) soon turned buccaneer-pirates.

An exception was Henry Morgan, a notorious pirate-turned-privateer. He was appointed to rally the notorious Jamaican buccaneers during the English war with Spain in 1668. Morgan went on to capture and destroy the Spanish South American capital at Panama. He then

CARIBBEAN

retired to his handsome estates in Jamaica, where he was elected Deputy Governor, and became the scourge of his former comrades.

True pirates of the Caribbean owed allegiance to no one. They

terrorized shipping from the Caribbean to North Carolina, occasional home of Edward Teach, better known as the notorious Blackbeard. Famed for roaring into battle with half a dozen pistols (three in each hand), and the pigtails of his beard spliced with lighted fuses, he was a frequent visitor to Port Royal, Jamaica, described in a London newspaper of the 1690s as the "dunghill of the universe." Other pirate hotspots included the Virgin Islands and the tricky seas and secluded cays of the Bahama Islands.

But the golden age of Caribbean piracy was nearing its end. Governor Woodes Rogers arrived to clear up the

Though many have searched for buccaneer gold, little has been found

Bahamas in 1718, the same year the British Navy caught up with Blackbeard. Defiant to the last, it is said Teach's decapitated body swam several laps around the ship before it sank. Calico Jack was surprised during a drunken revel in Jamaica, tried, hung, and buried on Rackham's Cay, off Kingston, in 1720. During the trial, two of his shipmates were discovered to be women, Anne Bonney and Mary Read, as ruthless a pair of bloodthirsty pirates as ever there was.

Guadeloupe and St. Barthélemy (St. Barts)

Shaped like a butterfly with two mismatched wings, the French-owned island of Guadeloupe is an unusual place. The western "wing," Basse-Terre, is mountainous, rain forested, and dominated by the steaming Soufrière volcano. Grande-Terre, the northeastern wing, is flat and dry, its white-sand southern beaches proving a magnet for the trappings of the tourist industry.

Sighted by Columbus in 1493, Guadeloupe was one of the "Cannibal Isles," and subsequently given a wide berth until 1635, when French settlers arrived to drive out the remaining Caribs. In terms of French priorities, the island played second string to

Martinique for years, though there was a brief moment of glory in 1794, when Guadeloupean *patriotes* overthrew the planters and installed a revolutionary government under Victor Hugues. (Martinique's planters and business-people steadfastly maintained the pre-Revolutionary status quo.) Guadeloupean slaves were freed, and Hugues erected the mandatory guillotine on the main square in Pointe-à-Pitre, where 300 enemies of the Revolution lost their heads. When Paris reintroduced slavery from 1802 until 1848, many freed Guadeloupean slaves preferred death to submission.

Guadeloupe has two cruise ports: the modest west coast capital of Basse-Terre and the busier commercial center of the island, Pointe-à-Pitre, located in the southeastern corner of Grande-Terre. From Basse-Terre, the Soufrière volcano is the most popular day trip. If you dock in Pointe-à-Pitre, you can opt for a day on the beach, or take a trip into Basse-Terre's Parc Naturel (see pages 88–9).

POINTE-À-PITRE

Guadeloupe's main cruise ship port and largest town, Pointe-à-Pitre is an unattractive port with congested streets

Guadeloupean girls dressed for the annual Lenten carnival

GUADELOUPE

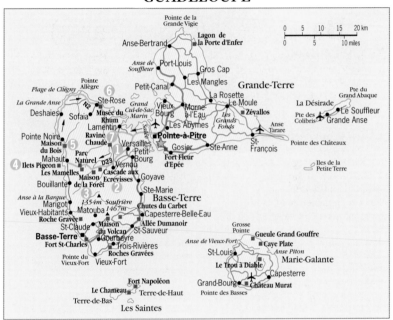

| | | | 0 | 5 | 10 | 15 | 20 km |

Pointe de la
Grande Vigie

Lagon de
la Porte d'Enfer

Anse-Bertrand

Anse de
Souffleur Port-Louis Gros Cap

Plage de Cligny Pointe Petit-Canal Les Mangles **Grande-Terre** Pte du
Allègre Grand Abaque
La Grande Anse Ste-Rose Grand La Rosette La Désirade Le Souffleur
Deshaies Cul-de-Sac Vieux Morne- Le Moule Pte des Grande Anse
Sofaïa Musée du Marin Bourg à-l'Eau Zévallos Colibris
Rhum Les Anse
Lamentin Les Abymes Grands Tarare
Pointe Noire Ravine **Pointe-à-Pitre** Fonds
Maison Chaude Versailles Gosier Ste-Anne St-
du Bois Parc Petit- François Pointe des Châteaux
Mahaut Naturel Bourg Fort Fleur
Ilets Pigeon Les Mamelles Vernou d'Epée Iles de la
Bouillante Cascade aux Goyave Petite Terre
Maison Ecrévisses
Anse à la Barque de la Forêt Ste-Marie
Marigot 1354m Soufrière **Basse-Terre**
Vieux-Habitants Matouba 1467m Capesterre-Belle-Eau
Roche Gravée Allée Dumanoir Grosse
St-Claude Maison St-Sauveur Pointe Gueule Grand Gouffre
Basse-Terre du Volcan Anse de Vieux-Fort Caye Plate
Fort St-Charles Gourbeyre St-Louis Anse Piton
Pointe du Trois-Rivières Marie-Galante
Vieux-Fort Roches Gravées Le Trou à Diable
Vieux-Fort Capesterre
Fort Napoléon Grand-Bourg Château Murat
Le Chameau Terre-de-Haut Pointe des Basses
Terre-de-Bas **Les Saintes**

and frenetic waterfront markets. However, you can relax in the cafés around place de la Victoire, the central gardens shaded by palm, mango, and African tulip trees, cooled by fountains, and edged by a clutch of venerable Colonial-style buildings.

Nearby, there is a small flower market outside the Cathedral of St. Peter and St. Paul, with its iron frame bolted together like an elaborate Meccano set. Close by, off rue Frébault, is a marvelous Covered Market, piled high with spices, sun hats, and staffed by garrulous lady vendors.

A short walk away on rue Peynier, a pretty pink French townhouse with wrought iron decorations and a double staircase houses the Musée Schoelcher.

Here, you will find assorted mementoes of the famous French abolitionist who led the fight against slavery in the 19th century, together with collections of African ivories, model ships, ceramics, and other curios.

Musée Schoelcher – open: Monday, Tuesday, Thursday, Friday, 8:30am– 12:30pm and 2–5:30pm, and Saturday morning. Admission charge.

Guadeloupe Office Departementale du Tourisme – 5 square de la Banque, 97163 Pointe-à-Pitre. Tel: (590) 82.09.30; also **St. Bart's Office Municipale du Tourisme** –quai Général de Gaulle, 97133 Gustavia. Tel: (590) 27.87.27.

Place St-François in the quiet Guadeloupean capital of Basse-Terre

GRANDE-TERRE

The main attractions on low-lying
Grande-Terre are its beaches, and the
best of these are found on the south coast
between Gosier and St.-François. Gosier
is the most touristy of the three seaside
towns along this stretch. Both Ste.-Anne
and St.-François are former fishing ports,
though most of the fishing these days is
done by tourists who enjoy the excellent
sport-fishing.

Fort Fleur d'Epée

Shaded by flaming Flamboyant (royal
poinciana) trees, midway between
Pointe-à-Pitre and Gosier, these 18th-
century coral rock fortifications afford
fine views across the bay to Gosier, down
the Basse-Terre coast to Pointe
Capesterre, and across to the islands of
Marie-Galante and La Désirade.
Open: daily, 9am–6pm. Free.

BASSE-TERRE

The administrative capital of
Guadeloupe is a small sleepy town
tucked in the lee of the central highlands,
about an hour's drive from Pointe-à-
Pitre. Founded in 1643, Basse-Terre has
several fine public buildings, a cathedral
dating back to the 17th century, and the
rambling ramparts of Fort St.-Charles,
on the southern edge of town. Founded
in 1650 and enlarged over the centuries,
the fort now houses a small local history
museum.
Museum – open: daily, 9am–5pm. Free.

CHUTES DU CARBET

Fed by the Grand Carbet River, which
originates in La Soufrière, these popular
waterfalls come in three stages. The 360-
foot-high second spill is the most easily
visited, just a 20-minute walk through
the rain forest.
Northwest of St.-Sauveur.

MAISON DU VOLCAN

Perched on the forested slopes of La
Soufrière above Basse-Terre, the Maison
du Volcan acts as an unofficial visitor
center for the volcano, providing a brief
introduction to vulcanism and the
region's origins. The setting up here on
the hill is lovely, there is an appreciable
drop in temperature, and you can see a
fair number of other old Creole-style
planter's houses nestled against the
hillside.
St.-Claude. Open: daily, 10am–6pm. Free.

ST. BARTHÉLEMY

PARC NATUREL DE GUADELOUPE

See pages 88–9.

LA SOUFRIÈRE

The highest point in the Eastern Caribbean at 4,318 feet (1,467m) above sea level, the sulphurous Soufrière crater is an eerie, nightmarish landscape of bubbling mud pools, bizarre lava formations, and wisps of steam. Eruptions and major earth movements were noted in 1695, 1797, 1837, 1956, and 1976. Vehicles can venture as far as the Savane à Mulets, 1,000 feet short of the crater. There are marked footpaths leading to the summit, and the uphill hike takes around two hours.

ST. BARTHÉLEMY

More commonly known as St. Barts, this pint-sized (9 square miles) volcanic dot lies 125 miles northwest of Guadeloupe. It is the most chic spot in the Caribbean, with exquisite beaches, exclusive shopping, and gourmet restaurants, which will delight style-conscious Francophiles, but not those on a budget.

First settled by French sailors from Brittany and Normandy, St. Barts spent

100 years under Swedish rule during the 18th and 19th centuries; hence the name of the capital, Gustavia. Catch up on the island history here at the Musée de St-Barth, on the west side of the harbor. And don't miss the delightful fishing village of Corossol, just north of Gustavia, a picture-book Breton community dropped into a tropical setting; some older ladies still wear traditional frilly starched Breton sunbonnets. The best beaches are on the south coast at Anse du Gouverneur and Anse de Grande Saline (no facilities); Anse des Flamands, in the north, has a couple of hotels. Remember, this is a French island, so topless bathing is *de rigueur*.

Musée de St.-Barth – open: Monday to Thursday, 8:30am–12:30pm, 2.30–6pm; Saturday, 8.30–noon. Free.

Mist hangs over the Chutes du Carbet waterfall in the rain forest

Guadeloupe

This 65-km circuit out of Pointe-à-Pitre around the northern tip of Basse-Terre (see map on page 85) takes in some spectacular rain forest scenery, a chance to visit one of Jacques Cousteau's top ten dive spots (by glass-bottomed boat) at Ilets Pigeon, and a spot of rum tasting. *Allow a generous ½-day (there is a suggested lunch stop at Deshaies, if time permits).*

1 ROUTE DE LA TRAVERSÉE

Once clear of Pointe-à-Pitre, this cross-island road skims westwards past sugarcane fields lined with tulip trees (stunning in July), before climbing up into the 74,000-acre Parc Naturel and crossing the Col des Mamelles. This pass affords stunning views of the aptly named twin volcanic peaks of Les Mamelles (The Breasts).

Marked trails encourage visitors to explore the 74,000-acre Parc Naturel

2 CASCADE AUX ECREVISSES

Just inside the Parc Naturel, this pretty waterfall gushes from the hillside near the road. It's a favorite picnic spot, and sure-footed explorers can scramble around the boulders along the river's edge.

3 MAISON DE LA FORÊT

The park information center is worth a stop to pick up brochures on the local flora and fauna. There is also a network of marked trails leading off into the lush rain forest.
At the end of the Route de la Traversée, turn south for Ilets Pigeon, or continue north on the main road.

4 ILETS PIGEON

Frequent glass-bottomed boat tours depart for short trips out to this tiny island reserve, just off the west coast. It is a bit of a detour, but the underwater panorama is spectacular, with visibility up to 80 feet, revealing superb corals and dazzling marine life.

A rain forest path just a short distance from the Maison de la Forêt

5 MAISON DU BOIS

Local woodcrafts of all descriptions are on display at this small museum in the cabinet-making center of Pointe Noire. Sections devoted to tools and domestic utensils from the pre-electric era include wicker lobster pots and hand-whisks, plus machines for seeding cotton, grinding coffee, and building wheels and boats. There is also a furniture showroom and a miniarboretum on the grounds.

Continue north to Deshaies, where there is a fine beach and a good Creole restaurant, Le Karacoli (see page 175). The coast-hugging route then winds on past the popular surfing beach at Clugny to Ste-Rose.

6 MUSÉE DU RHUM (MUSEUM OF RUM)

An exhaustive and detailed history of rum (with English translations) is enlivened by some evocative turn-of-the-century photographs of local merchants and craftspeople. These candid shots of the laundress and the sorbet maker, the milk ladies and the fish trap workers are reason enough to visit, but rum-lovers will also be offered an opportunity to sample the product after viewing a short film and taking a look at the various exhibits. A juice vat hewn out of a single tree trunk is particularly impressive.

The road runs inland from Ste-Rose back to the Route de la Traversée. If you are short of time, return direct to Pointe-à-Pitre. Otherwise, there is one last detour at Lamentin.

7 RAVINE CHAUDE

The sulphurous natural hot springs at Lamentin are reputed to have healing and recuperative powers (especially after a long drive). But even if you do not fancy a dip, this is a good place to stretch your legs and enjoy a refreshing glass of punch before returning to the ship.

Take the N2 back to Pointe-à-Pitre.

Maison de la Forêt – open: Monday to Saturday, 9am–5pm. Free.
Maison du Bois – open: daily, 9am–6pm. Admission charge.
Musée du Rhum – open: Monday to Saturday, 9am–5pm. Admission charge.

Jamaica

Seven hundred miles south of Miami, Jamaica is the third largest of the Caribbean islands (4,411 square miles) and a natural beauty, with jungle-clad mountains, rushing rivers, and superb beaches. Christopher Columbus reckoned it to be "the fairest island that eyes have beheld," Noël Coward, Errol Flynn, Ian Fleming (author of the *James Bond* novels), and a host of other famous, and not-so-famous, devotees have lived here or found themselves returning time and time again, captivated by the island's physical beauty and the easy-going charm of its people.

When Columbus first landed here in 1494, the island was called Xaymaca (Land of Wood and Water) by the peaceable Arawak Indians who inhabited it. The first permanent Spanish settlement was founded on the north coast in 1510, and the Arawaks were forced into slavery. Within a century, the estimated native population of around 100,000 had been tragically wiped out. Many fell victim to European diseases, others were hunted for sport.

The British captured Jamaica from Spain in 1655, and set about turning the island into the world's largest sugar producer, using thousands of West African slaves who were bought and sold at the slave market in Kingston. From the latter part of the 17th century up until the abolition of slavery in 1834, the colonists flourished. And more than a few of them (such as Henry Morgan) made the switch to the "respectable" and luxurious planter's lifestyle after earning their fortunes on the high seas as buccaneers.

Some slaves managed to escape and hide in the inaccesible mountain territory of Cockpit Country, in the central west highlands. Known as *maroons*, they waged a sporadic guerrilla war against the planters and government. The most

Jamaica Tourist Board – PO Box 67, Gloucester Avenue, Cornwall Beach, Montego Bay. Tel: (876) 952 4425; PO Box 240, Ocean Village Shopping Center, Ocho Rios. Tel: (809) 974 2582; **Kingston Tourism Center** – PO Box 360, 2 St. Lucia Avenue, Kingston. Tel: (876) 929 9200.

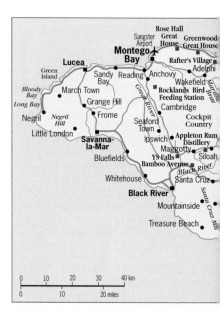

Another stunning Jamaican sunset on one of the Caribbean's most beautiful islands

famous slave revolt was led by Sam Sharpe in 1831, and even today he is regarded as a national hero. Finally, in 1834, the Emancipation Act gave freedom to all slaves, though this only became reality after a subsequent 4-year tied "apprenticeship" period to their plantation. Former slaves claimed what land they could and turned to agriculture with the help of Christian missionaries. A century of political experimentation and the growing 1930s nationalist movement led to the creation of trade unions, political parties, and a new constitution in 1944. Jamaica was the first British colony in the Caribbean to achieve independence, in 1962.

Jamaica's two main cruise ports are on the north coast, at Montego Bay and Ocho Rios, though some cruise lines also use Port Antonio farther east and the south coast island capital, Kingston.

JAMAICA

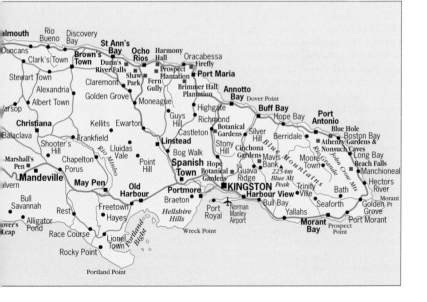

Bob Marley (1945–81), international reggae star and Jamaican national hero

KINGSTON

The island's capital since 1872, Kingston sprang up after the old buccaneering base of Port Royal slid into the sea as a result of an earthquake and tidal wave in 1692. Today, this is the seat of government and business and boasts a population of over one million.

Kingston lacks charm but offers a handful of cultural attractions. A favorite escape from the downtown maelstrom is the cheap ferry ride across the harbor to the former site of Port Royal, where the ramparts of Fort Charles afford views back to the Blue Mountains. There is also a clutch of small maritime and history museums.

Bob Marley Museum

Reggae music fans will want to make tracks to this memorial to Trench Town's most famous son, displayed in the former Tuff Gong recording studio. *56 Hope Road. Tel: (876) 927 9152. Open: Monday to Friday, 9.30am–4.30pm. Admission charge.*

Devon House

A restored 19th-century great house, with a touristy collection of craft stalls and souvenir shops in the stables. The interior boasts fine antique furnishings. *26 Hope Road. Tel: (876) 929 6602. Open: Tuesday to Saturday, 10am–5pm. Admission charge.*

Hope Botanical Gardens

Established in 1881, these 200-acre botanical gardens provide an explosion of marvelous color, shady paths,

THE BLUE MOUNTAINS

Crowded into the eastern corner of the island, the spectacular Blue Mountains soar up to Blue Mountain Peak, which tops 7,402 feet (2,254m). The climb begins the minute you leave Kingston in a tortuous, winding squiggle all the way north along the Wag River to the Castleton Botanical Gardens, or northwest to the Cinchona Gardens at a breathtaking 5,500 feet. With a bird's-eye view of three deeply etched river valleys below, the Cinchona Gardens were originally laid out as a tea and cinchona plantation in 1868 (the bark of cinchona is used to make the anti-malaria drug quinine). The region is now noted for the Blue Mountain coffee, reckoned by aficionados to be the best in the world. If you count yourself among them, make a visit to one of the coffee factories at Silver Hill or Mavis Bank during the harvesting season (September to February), watch the berries being processed, and purchase a hoard of the aromatic beans to take home.

modern Jamaican art world include David Pottinger, Ralph Campbell, and sculptors Christopher Gonzalez and Edna Manley.
Orange Street (at Ocean Boulevard). Tel: (876) 922 1561. Open: Monday to Friday, 11am–4.30pm. Admission charge.

Spanish Town

The original capital of Jamaica for over 300 years, Spanish Town lies 14 miles west of Kingston. Though founded by the Spanish in 1523, the colonial-style Georgian stone buildings lend a distinctly British air to the town center, where British naval hero Admiral Rodney (inexplicably attired in Roman garb) strikes a commanding pose over the main square, known as The Park. On The Park, a former governor's residence, the Kings House, is home to a museum of folk crafts and colonial period furnishings, while 3 miles east on the road to Kingston, the White Marl Arawak Museum pays tribute to Jamaica's earliest inhabitants.
King's House – open: Monday to Saturday, 9am–5pm. Free. White Marl Arawak Museum – open: Monday to Friday, 10am–4pm. Admission charge.

sweeping lawns, and elegant royal palms. There's also a restaurant and children's zoo to visit.
Old Hope Road. Tel: (876) 927 1257. Open: daily, 8:30am–6:30pm. Free to park; admission charge to zoo.

National Gallery of Art

This is one of the best permanent displays of Caribbean art in the region, rich in oil paintings, drawings, sculpture, and wood carvings. Notable names in the

Colonial-style Devon House, Kingston

Doctor's Cave Beach was a fashionable health resort in the early 1900s

GREENWOOD GREAT HOUSE

This was the Barrett family home, built by a relative of poet Elizabeth Barrett Browning in the early 19th century. Superb antique furnishings, musical instruments, and restored carriages evoke the gracious plantation lifestyle.
16 miles east of Montego Bay. Tel: (876) 953 1077. Open: daily, 9am–6pm. Admission charge.

ROCKLAND BIRD FEEDING STATION

Perched in the hills in the settlement of Anchovy, this is a great chance to get close to Jamaica's diverse and beautiful bird life. Hundreds of darting, chattering birds gather for the afternoon feeding sessions, first initiated by "bird lady" Lisa Salmon, in 1958. Many of the diners are tame enough to feed from your hand.
9 miles south of Montego Bay. Tel: (876) 952 2009. Open: daily, 2–5pm. Admission charge.

MONTEGO BAY

"Mo' Bay" is Jamaica's second largest town, but number one in the island's tourism stakes. "Montego" is derived from the Spanish *manteca*, meaning pig fat, from the days when sailors would come ashore here to hunt wild hogs. At the turn of the century, it became fashionable to bathe at Doctor's Cave Beach, and the rest, as they say, is history.

Sam Sharpe Square, at the heart of town, is a short taxi ride from the cruise ship dock, where the tourist office is housed in The Cage, a former lockup for slaves and drunks. The area around Montego Bay offers plenty of attractions, many of which can be covered by shore excursions.

APPLETON RUM DISTILLERY

Up in the hills of Cockpit Country, the Appleton Estate produces Jamaica's most famous rum. After a tour of the distillery, there are tastings and an opportunity to blend your own personal rum.
Siloah. Open: Monday to Friday, 9am–4pm. Admission charge.

RAFTING ON THE MARTHA BRAE

A river trip is just the ticket for a sweltering day, so take along your swimsuit for a 90-minute raft ride down the gentle Martha Brae River, near Falmouth. Once clear of Rafters' Village (a distinctly tourist-orientated affair with shops, refreshments, and a swimming pool), the two-person, 30-foot bamboo rafts glide past tropical scenery, with only the birds and butterflies for company.
Rafters' Village, 26 miles south of Montego Bay. Tel: (876) 954 5168. Raft rental daily, 9am–4pm.

ROSE HALL GREAT HOUSE

The most famous house in Jamaica – possibly the whole Caribbean – largely by virtue of its legendary mistress, Annie Palmer, who was also known as the "White Witch of Rose Hall." The 19th-century *femme fatale* is (falsely) credited with bumping off three husbands and numerous slave lovers before being murdered in her bed. Guides in period dress lay it on thick as you tour the restored interior.

8 miles east of Montego Bay. Tel: (876) 953 2323. Open: daily, 9:30am–6pm. Admission charge.

PORT ANTONIO

Founded in 1723, this is the resort that time forgot – almost. Built on a point dividing two stunning bays, with the Blue Mountains in the background, Port Antonio's setting is truly fabulous. A booming banana boat port and resort at the turn of the century, the town's fortunes took a dive. Though the swashbuckling Errol Flynn bought Navy Island and turned it into a Hollywood hideaway for his fellow stars in the 1940s and '50s, Port Antonio has never fully recovered top resort status – many of the buildings look very tired. However, at least the town is mercifully free of the high-rise developments characterized by Montego Bay or Ocho Rios.

The local sights are pretty low key, starting with the stunning Blue Hole (better known as Hollywood's Blue Lagoon). The Nonsuch Caves offer bizarre rock formations; there are raft trips on the Rio Grande and tours into the Blue Mountains (see page 93).

A peak hour log-jam as tourists glide down the Martha Brae (see box opposite)

Dunn's River Falls Beach on Jamaica's central north coast

EXCURSIONS AROUND OCHO RIOS

Midway along the north coast, 65 miles east of Montego Bay, the former fishing village of Ocho Rios has been given the full mass tourism development treatment and emerged as a seamless chain of hotels and burger franchises fringed by packed beaches. This is also Jamaica's busiest cruise ship destination. Duty-free shopping is within striking distance of the pier, but unless you want to spend the rest of the day on the beach, you will need transportation to reach any of the local attractions.

COBAYA RIVER GARDEN AND MUSEUM

The name comes from the Arawak word for "paradise," and the museum occupies the grounds of the old Shaw Park Hotel, in turn built on the site of an ancient Amerindian settlement. It traces Jamaica's history and cross-cultural influences, from the Arawaks and Spanish, through the colonial period, right up to the present day. National heroes, such as Marcus Garvey and Bob Marley, take their place alongside art and architecture exhibits. Take time to admire the gardens, investigate the gallery, and relax over a cup of home-grown Blue Mountain coffee.
Shaw Park Estate, 2½ miles east of Ocho Rios. Open: daily, 8:30am–5pm. Admission charge.

DUNN'S RIVER FALLS

Probably the single most popular outing for every visitor to the island, these deliciously cool mountain falls tumble 600 feet down to the sea over a series of easily climbable ledges. Check in your clothes and valuables at the ticket entrance lockers, and join the swimsuit-clad "daisy chain" (a human conga line rallied by sure-footed guides), on the slippery route to the top. The ascent takes about 40 minutes.
Off the A1, 2 miles west of Ocho Rios. Tel: (876) 974 2857. Open: daily, 8am–5pm. Admission charge.

FIREFLY

Playwright and professional wit Noël Coward purchased this magnificent 1,000-foot-high crow's nest site in the 1940s, and must have spent much of his

A "daisy chain" ascends the slippery boulders of Dunn's River Falls

last 23 years admiring the incredible views. In fact, it's such a good lookout that buccaneer Henry Morgan is reputed to have used the tumbledown limestone building below the house as a shore retreat.

The interior of Firefly has been meticulously restored, right down to Coward's silk pajamas hanging in the wardrobe. There are paintings, photographs, and other memorabilia, plus a chance to enjoy cucumber sandwiches and Earl Grey tea on the veranda. Coward is buried in the garden, beneath a plain marble tomb.
Off the A3, 21 miles east of Ocho Rios. Tel: (876) 997 7201. Open: Monday to Saturday, 9am–4pm. Admission charge.

HARMONY HALL

This attractively restored late 18th-century "gingerbread" country house makes an inviting gallery for the works of contemporary Jamaican artists. Visiting exhibitions are a feature, and souvenir-hunters will find a good range of top-quality craft items. There is also a bar, restaurant, and garden terrace.
Off the A3, 4 miles east of Ocho Rios. Tel: (876) 974 4478. Open: daily, 10am–6pm. Free.

PROSPECT PLANTATION

The 1,000-acre Prospect estate is one of Jamaica's finest working plantations, cultivating bananas, cassava, cocoa, pawpaws, pimentos, and sugarcane among other crops. Entertaining narrated tours aboard an old-fashioned

jitney (canopied open wagon) take around an hour, and include dramatic views of the White River Gorge, a stop at Sir Harold's Viewpoint for a panoramic vista of the coast, and an avenue of trees planted by such famous visitors as Charlie Chaplin and Sir Winston Churchill. If you want to do some horse-back riding, call in advance and they will have a suitable steed awaiting you on your arrival.
Off the A3, 4 miles east of Ocho Rios. Tel: (876) 974 2058. Open: daily for tours at 10:30am, 2pm, and 3:30pm. Admission charge.

A former admiral's home, the century-old DeMontevin Lodge is now a hotel

Martinique

Martinique is renowned for the beauty of its flora, its beaches, and its people – though not necessarily in that order. The island was spotted by Columbus on either his second or fourth trip, but not settled until 1635. Apart from a couple of brief foreign incursions during the 18th century, Martinique has remained indisputably French, and indeed is a fully-fledged *région* of France. French is the first (and often only) language, and the French franc is the local currency.

Martinique is one of the larger islands in the Lesser Antilles (measuring 62 miles by 23 miles), so plan your time ashore with care. A visit to the mountainous green heart of the island, dominated by the ominous volcanic bulk of Mont Pelée, is a must, while the capital, Fort-de-France, is a shopper's delight. To the south, rippling cane fields stretch off to the horizon behind some of those famous beaches.

FORT-DE-FRANCE

Clambering up the steep hillsides behind the Baie des Flamands, the capital's narrow streets pack closely around the attractive 12-acre Savane gardens on the harbor. Facing the top left-hand corner, the runaway Byzantine-Egyptian Art Nouveau Bibliothéque Schoelcher was

> **JOSÉPHINE**
> An 18th-century Martiniquan fortune-teller once read the palms of two cousins on the island and foretold that one would become an empress, the other "more than an empress." The former became Napoleon's Empress Joséphine. Her simple childhood home, La Pagerie, can be visited near Les Trois-Ilets (16 miles south of Fort-de-France). The other was kidnapped by Barbary pirates and taken to Istanbul, where she became the Turkish sultan's favorite concubine, the Sultana Validé.

built for the 1889 Paris Exposition, and transported here piece by piece. It is named after Victor Schoelcher, a leading light in the 19th-century movement to abolish slavery. The Musée Départemental de Martinique, at 9 rue de la Liberté, houses exhibits on slavery and colonial life and some notable pre-Columbian artifacts. Behind rue de la Liberté, the main shopping district is bordered by rue Victor-Hugo and rue Victor-Sévère. The Cathédrale St-Louis is here too, on rue Schoelcher.

If the beach is your prime objective,

Capital of Martinique, Fort-de-France exudes a distinctly Gallic air

there is a convenient ferry service from the waterfront to four of the best beaches close to the capital. Plage Pointe du Bout offers a human-made strip of white sand lined with luxury hotels; Plage Anse-Mitan is also well-supplied with hotels and beach bars and has good snorkeling; the narrow sandy crescent of Plage Anse à l'Ane has plenty of shade and a couple of small hotel-restaurants; while Plage Grande-Anse is the most basic with piles

of fishing nets, laid-back beach bars, and boats for rent.

Musée Départemental de Martinique – open: Monday to Friday, 8.30am–1pm, 2.30–5pm; Saturday, 9am–noon. Admission charge.

Martinique Office du Tourisme – rue Ernest Deproge, Fort-de-France. Tel: (596) 63.79.60.

MARTINIQUE

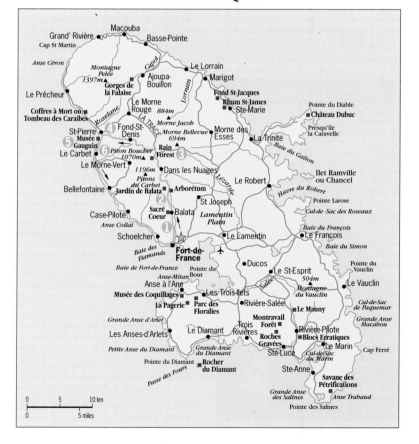

Northern Martinique

An excursion into the spectacular Martinique rain forest should be one of the scenic highlights of any Caribbean trip. The initial leg of this route (see map on page 99) from Fort-de-France follows La Trace, an inland forest road to St-Pierre, first carved through the undergrowth by Jesuits in the 17th century. *Allow 3 to 4 hours.*

1 SACRÉ COEUR

Martinique's mini version of the great Parisian landmark, Sacré-Coeur

One glimpse at the "*Montmartre martiniquais*" and you could be forgiven for thinking you are hallucinating. This minireplica of the famous Parisian basilica was erected in 1923 as a memorial to the dead of World War I.

2 JARDIN DE BALATA

These glorious gardens are not to be missed. Massed hibiscus, poinsettias, bougainvillaea, and plumes of red ginger glow in the sunlight; swathes of strange, glossy anthurium and pink torch ginger sprawl in the shade. All around are ferns, flamboyant (royal poinciana) trees, fruit trees, spice bushes, and variegated immortelles. And then there are the hummingbirds zipping around the bottle-brush bushes.

3 THE RAIN FOREST

From Balata, the winding road continues up into the Pitons du Carbet, lined by a living curtain of ferns, elephant ears, bamboo, and feathery palms sprouting bromeliads. Banana plantations cover the hillsides leading down to the coast.

4 ST.-PIERRE

Once the "Paris of the Antilles," St.-Pierre overlooks a splendid bay in the shadow of Mont Pelée. Old photographs show the harbor filled with clipper ships,

The Musée Gauguin at Anse Turin also displays work by local artists

and fashionable young women strolling beneath their parasols along paved streets. In the spring of 1902, after centuries of silence, Mont Pelée began to grumble. On May 5, the side of the crater split and released a stream of mud and lava, but local officials in the midst of an election campaign decided not to issue warnings. The Governor arrived on May 7, and urged people to leave, but only about 1,000 took his advice.

Just before 8am on May 8, the volcano erupted. In advance of the lava, a cloud of burning ash and poisonous gas reaching temperatures over 3,700°F swept down over the town and into the sea where it caused the water to boil. Thirty thousand Pierrotins were asphyxiated and carbonized within minutes. Miraculously, there was one survivor, Auguste Cyparis, who was in the underground town jail.

St.-Pierre never recovered, and its present-day population of 6,000 live among the gaunt reminders of the cataclysmic eruption. You can explore freely around the ruins of the theater, Cyparis' cell, and the rebuilt cathedral (only the façade survived). The before-and-after photographs in the Musée Vulcanologique, together with fused musket balls, melted glass bottles, and other curios are well worth a look.
Follow the coast road south towards Fort-de-France.

5 MUSÉE GAUGUIN

The 19th-century French painter Paul Gauguin stayed on the beach here at Anse Turin for five months as he searched the Caribbean for a spot where he could live as a "noble savage." He eventually wound up in Tahiti; but not before writing the handful of complaining letters to his long-suffering wife, displayed here with reproductions of his paintings.
Continue south to Le Carbet.

6 LE CARBET

This is said to be the spot where Columbus came ashore on his fourth voyage to the New World, in 1502. French settler Pierre Belain d'Esnambuc and one hundred fellow Norman colonists definitely landed here, in 1635.
Return to Fort-de-France.

Jardin de Balata – open: daily, 9am–5pm. Admission charge.
Musée Vulcanologique – rue Victor Hugo. Open: daily, 9am–5pm. Admission charge.

SLAVERY

The first Negro ever to set eyes on the Caribbean was Pedro Alonzo Niño. He was not a slave, but the navigator aboard the caravel *Niña*, one of three ships Christopher Columbus took on his first voyage to the New World.

The slave trade between West Africa and Europe was established by this time and was, in fact, inspired by the Africans themselves. Domestic slavery of captured enemies was accepted practice amongst African tribes, and they in turn sold their slaves to the Europeans in exchange for manufactured goods, such as textiles, glass,

and weapons.

As South America and the West Indies were colonized, and the native Indian population (the very first Caribbean slaves) was decimated by disease and ill-treatment, the search began for a replacement workforce to dig gold mines and tend the tobacco and sugar plantations.

The result was the infamous "triangular trade." Manufactured goods were shipped from Europe to be exchanged for West African slaves. The living cargo was then transported in appalling conditions on the notorious Middle Passage to the New World, where the ships were loaded with raw materials – sugar, spices, cotton,

Contemporary prints and paintings present a stylized (and sanitized) view of slavery

tobacco, and rum – for Europe. It has been estimated that during the 250-year heyday of the Caribbean slave trade, as many as 40 million Africans were transported to the West Indies, the largest forced transportation of human beings in history. One in eight died on the Middle Passage.

Conditions were little better for the survivors on arrival. Sold at auction like animals, slaves were then "seasoned" with brutal discipline. Beatings, brandings, and the frequent use of neck chains, leg irons, and other torturous devices were common. To further break their spirit and ties to African culture, families were split up, and slaves were forbidden to speak in their native tongue. They worked 18-hour days, and children as young as five were put to work weeding and picking cane.

Contemporary records show that up to thirty percent of the slave population died every 4 years.

It was economics, not morals, that finally put an end to the slave trade. There were heroic abolitionists without doubt – Granville Sharp, Thomas Clarkson, and William Wilberforce in Britain, Victor Schoelcher in France among them. But the introduction of sugar beet in Europe made the colonial trade less viable, and in 1838 (four years after the Emancipation Act) abolition finally became a reality in Britain. France followed suit in 1848.

Netherlands Antilles

*T*he Dutch were important traders during the colonial era and secured six possessions in the Caribbean: three in the Windward Islands and three in the Leewards. Sint Maarten in the Windwards is shared with France (see page 122). The remaining Windward Islands, Saba and St. Eustatius (known as "Statia"), can only be visited by the very smallest cruise ships. Largely undeveloped, they remain rare oases of tranquility. Five hundred miles due south, the Dutch Leeward Islands of Bonaire, Curaçao, and self-governing Aruba (the ABC islands) lie off the coast of Venezuela.

ARUBA

This low-lying, scrubby island, some 20 miles by 6 miles, had inauspicious beginnings. It was claimed by Spain in 1499, but subsequently rejected as an *isla inutila* (useless island), and it was ignored for over 100 years until the Dutch West Indies Company developed Curaçao. Aruba and neighboring Bonaire proved useful for salt production and as ranches for cattle and horses. Few slaves were ever employed on the island, and it is therefore one of the rare places native Amerindians survived *in situ*, as can be witnessed in the faces of the local

Jaunty color schemes, Dutch gables, and stucco decoration in downtown Oranjestad

populace. The discovery of offshore oil in the 1920s led to an economic boom, until declining prices turned the island towards tourism in the 1980s.

Though no longer technically a part of the Netherlands Antilles since gaining autonomy in 1986, Aruba remains within the Kingdom of the Netherlands.

Oranjestad

Behind a cordon of duty-free shopping malls, old-town Oranjestad (pronounced *Oran-yeh-stat*) is fun to explore. Some of the best examples of Dutch Colonial architecture are found along Wilhelminastraat. Overlooking the bay, 18th-century Fort Zoutman houses local history exhibits in the Museo Arubano.

Characteristically Dutch, the oldest building in Willemstad dates from 1708

The Archaeology Museum, J.E.Irausquinplein 2A (near the post office), displays Amerindian relics.
Museo Arubano – open: Monday to Saturday, 10am–noon, 1.30–4.30pm. Admission charge.
Archaeology Museum – open: Monday to Friday, 8am–noon, 1.30–4pm. Free.

Exploring Aruba

A taxi tour of the island takes just a couple of hours. Natural points of interest include the 541-foot-high Hooiberg (Haystack Hill) lookout point and the Casibara and Ayo rock formations in the center of the island. On the north coast, the sea has carved the dramatic 100-foot-long, 25-foot-high coral rock Natural Bridge near Noordkaap, and there are huge dunes at Boca Prins. To the southeast, you can visit the ruins of the Balashi Gold Mine (some say the name "Aruba" came from the Carib Indian words *ora uba*, meaning "gold was here"). The most spectacular beaches, Eagle and Palm, edge the west coast north of Oranjestad.

Netherlands Antilles: Aruba Tourist Authority Board – PO Box 1019, 172 L G Smith Boulevard, Oranjestad. Tel: (297) 8223777;
Curaçao Tourism Development Bureau – PO Box 3266, Pietermaai 19, Willemstad.
Tel: (599) 8616000.

NETHERLANDS ANTILLES

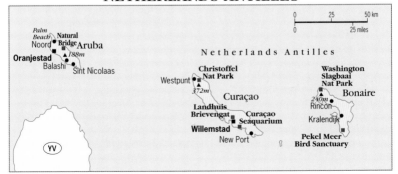

Learner divers train in the hotel pool before exploring dive sites off Bonaire

half-a-dozen European, South American, and African tongues. To all appearances, Curaçao remains an exotic hybrid, a slice of picture-book Dutch in a spaghetti-Western setting, complete with cacti and tortured-looking divi-divi trees with branches forced back at 45 degrees due southwest by the cooling *Passatwinden* (tradewinds). Fans of the great outdoors should make for the arid but dramatic scenery of the Christoffel National Park (see page 147).

BONAIRE

Like Saba and Statia, only small cruise ships visit Bonaire. Most visitors come here for the diving, which is some of the best in the world. Kralendijk is the island capital, with a population of 1,500. There's duty-free shopping on Breedestraat and a 19th-century fortress, Fort Oranje, which houses a small folklore museum. Around the island, there are salt pans in the south; and the 22-acre Washington Slagbaai National Park in the north is notable for its bird life. Most of Bonaire's superb coral dive sites are off the protected leeward side of the island, easily accessible from Kralendijk.

Folklore Museum – open: Monday to Friday, 8am–noon, 1–5pm. Free.

CURAÇAO

This is the largest of the Netherlands Antilles (measuring 38 miles by 9 miles) with a fine natural harbor. The Dutch landed on Curaçao in 1634, and swiftly transformed this strategically placed island into a major trading center for European and South American merchants. Curaçao flourished, attracting a polyglot community who in turn developed *Papiamento*, the bizarre local dialect with strains of more than

Willemstad

The cruise ship visitor's introduction to Curaçao's capital, and one of the prettiest sights in the Caribbean, Willemstad's pastel-painted waterfront, the Handelskade, is a delight. It is said a 19th-century governor first ordered the use of colored paints on the red-roofed, gabled buildings because the dazzling whitewash was hurting his eyes. Today, it is a major tourist attraction.

Cruise ships dock in the Otrabanda quarter within walking distance of the town center, the Punda, which is reached by the Queen Emma Bridge. (There is a free ferry when the 555-foot pontoon bridge is open.) On the waterfront, the late 17th-century Fort Amsterdam is now the governor's residence, and there's a floating market where Venezuelan schooners unload fruit and vegetables. On Columbusstraat, the Mikveh Israel-Emmanuel Synagogue is the oldest temple in the Americas. Founded in 1651, then rebuilt in the 18th century, it also has a small museum. For a bit of island history, return to the Otrabanda district and the Curaçao Museum on Van Leeuwenhoekstraat, which displays

Amerindian and colonial relics in a restored former seamen's hospital.
Mikveh Israel-Emmanuel Synagogue museum – open: Monday to Friday, 9–11:45am; 2:30–4.45pm. Admission charge.
Curaçao Museum – open: Monday to Friday, 9am–noon, 2–5pm; Sunday 10am–4pm. Admission charge.

Curaçao Liqueur Distillery

The Curaçao Liqueur Distillery, which occupies an old *landhuis* (country house) on the outskirts of town is a favorite stop for tour buses. A staple ingredient of any good cocktail bar, this famous sticky liqueur, which is produced from the peel of small, green oranges, comes in as many shades as the Willemstad waterfront, from the original orange to electric blue.
Open: Monday to Friday, 8am–noon, 1–5pm. Free.

Old-World charm and modern-day comfort meet in Willemstad, Curaçao's capital

Curaçao Seaquarium

The wonders of the deep (and not-so-deep) are superbly displayed in picture-window tanks. Included are more than 400 varieties of local marine life, from fish to corals and sponges. Glass-bottomed boats sail out to the reef, and there is a safe swimming beach here, too.
3½ miles east of Willemstad. Tel: (599) 461 6666. Open: daily, 9am–10pm. Admission charge.

LANDHUISEN
It is reckoned that there were around 300 plantations on Curaçao by the 19th century, most of them with a fine country house on the grounds. Eighty of these houses remain, of which around one third have been restored. A real highlight of any trip to Curaçao is a visit to the 18th-century Landhuis Brievengat, just north of Willemstad.
Open: Monday to Friday, 9.15am–12.15 and 3–6pm. Admission charge.

Puerto Rico

A thousand miles southeast of Miami, Puerto Rico is the smallest of the four Greater Antilles islands, measuring around 110 miles by 35 miles. Roughly rectangular in shape, it rises steeply from the developed coastal plains to a mountainous interior, formed by the spine of the Cordillera Central, cloaked in lush tropical rain forest.

Arawak Indians called the island *Borinquen*, but Columbus arrogantly renamed it San Juan Bautista, in 1493. Ponce de León, the discoverer of Florida, led the first group of Spanish settlers in 1508. He admired the *puerto rico* (rich port) of San Juan Bay, and within a few years the island and the main settlement exchanged names. The Spanish held the island for 400 years, surviving hurricanes and frequent attacks by pirates and plunderers, such as Sir Francis Drake, who sneaked past the town's defenses to torch the Spanish fleet anchored in the harbor. Puerto Rican hopes for

independence in the 19th century were dashed when Spain handed the island to the U.S. at the end of the Spanish-American War in 1898. In 1917, U.S. citizenship was granted to Puerto Ricans, and the country is now a Commonwealth of the U.S. with an elected parliament run on the U.S. model.

The American influence is highly visible in the daily life of San Juan and tourist areas, where English is widely spoken. Air-conditioned skyscrapers, chain hotels, American automobiles, fast food restaurants, and advertising are visible evidence of almost a century of

PUERTO RICO

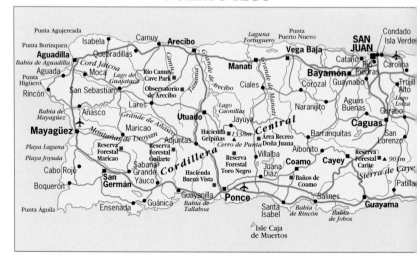

San Juan Bay, christened *puerto rico* (rich port) by Christopher Columbus

U.S. presence. However, the Puerto Ricans are proud and protective of their Latin origins. Catholicism, fiestas, the evening *paseo* (a pre-dinner stroll), and the clack of dominoes from *bodegas* and *tapas* bars lend Latin flavor to the streets of Old San Juan and quiet country villages.

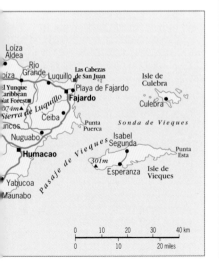

LELOLAI
If you are staying over in San Juan at the beginning or end of your cruise, one way to experience Latin vitality and verve is a Puerto Rican country music and dance show. The LeLoLai folkloric performances celebrate centuries of European and Afro-Antillean rhythms and culture, and are staged at several San Juan hotels. For information and reservations (tel: (787) 723 3135).

Puerto Rico Tourism Company Information Center – La Casita, Calle Comercio, Old Town San Juan. Tel: (787) 722 1709.

The massive fortifications of San Felipe del Morro fortress in Old San Juan

SAN JUAN

The original Puerto Rico was well-named. It is now one of the world's top cruise destinations, home to more than twenty cruise ships, who disgorge over a million passengers every year. The pier is conveniently located a few minutes' walk from Old San Juan, a real slice of old colonial Spain, with pretty balconied houses painted in yellow, white, fondant pink, powder blue, and pistachio green. Some streets are paved with blue-grey bricks transported as ballast in ships bound from Spain. On the return voyage, these same ships would be loaded with treasures plundered from South America.

The settlement was actually founded in 1520, and construction of the great El Morro fortress on the western peninsula began 20 years later. The growing town was enclosed by 30-foot-thick fortified walls punctuated by round stone sentry posts called *garitas*. The modern city has expanded beyond the walls; east along the Atlantic coast to the modern hotel and beach resorts of Condado and Isla Verde; south to the university district of Rio Piedras; and west around the bay to Catano, where the Bacardi Rum Plant offers tours and tastings.

OLD TOWN TROLLEYS

A good way to get your bearings and see the sights is aboard the free open-sided trolley buses that make narrated circuits of Old San Juan between 6:30am and 6:30pm. You can pick one up where you see the yellow *Parada* signs. There is a pick-up point outside the bus terminal, near the cruise ship pier.

Within the compact Old Town area, the main shopping streets are Calle Fortaleza and Calle San Francisco, while a good place to find typical Spanish-style bars and restaurants is the area around Plaza de San José. The main sights are covered in the walk around Old San Juan (see pages 112–13).
Bacardi Rum Plant – open: Monday to Saturday, 9:30am–3:30pm. Free.

Fort San Cristóbal
At the northeastern corner of the Old Town, this imposing 17th-century fort sprawls over a 27-acre site, bordered by five bastions fitted with cannons trained over the Atlantic approaches. There is an interesting scale model in the museum, and the Devil's Sentry Box is home to a resident ghostly sentry.
Calle Norzagaray. Tel: (787) 729 6960. Open: daily, 9am–5pm. Admission charge.

LUQUILLO BEACH
This magnificent stretch of golden sand on the eastern Atlantic coast sweeps around a bay lapped by inviting turquoise waters. There is plenty of shade beneath tropical palms, while beach bars sell fresh coconut milk, piña coladas, soft taco rolls filled with crab or lobster, *alcapurrias* (big banana fritters), and other delicious temptations. Quite simply – paradise!
Route 3, 30 miles east of San Juan.

RIO CAMUY CAVE PARK
A popular day trip, the Cave Park offers tours into a 170-foot-high subterranean cavern adorned with monster stalagmites and stalactites. It is part of one of the biggest cave networks in the Americas, and there are views of the River Camuy, one of the world's largest underground rivers.
Route 129 (KM18.9), Lares. Tel: (787) 898 3100. Open: Wednesday to Sunday, 8am–4pm. Admission charge.

EL YUNQUE (CARIBBEAN NATIONAL FOREST)
More than 100 billion gallons of rainwater fall on El Yunque (The Anvil) every year, so be prepared. However, all this precipitation has created a spectacular, rampant rain forest containing over 240 native species, including vines, epiphytes, giant ferns, and a variety of brilliant flowers. The fauna is almost equally impressive, including the rare Puerto Rican parrot. Look for brilliant blue wings, a red forehead, and green plumage.
Route 191, 40 miles east of San Juan.

Puerto Ricans take to the streets in style at carnival time

Old San Juan

The best way to appreciate Old San Juan is on foot. In addition to the major sights, there are numerous pretty streets, houses bedecked with window boxes and decorative iron grilles, and several welcoming refreshment stops. *Allow a minimum of 3 hours, with stops.*

Start at La Casita.

1 LA CASITA

This little pink house, formerly the Customs House, is now home to the tourist office. Proceed down the Paseo de la Princesa, below the Old Town walls. The Raices Fountain overlooking the harbor pays homage to the Taino Indian (Arawak), Spanish, and African influences on Puerto Rican culture.

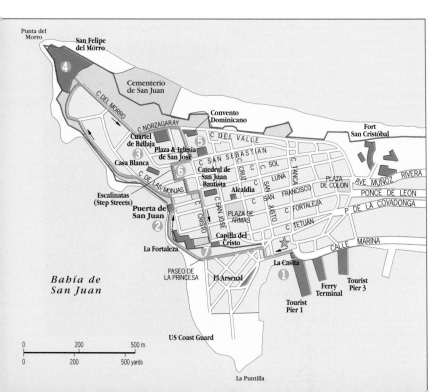

2 PUERTA DE SAN JUAN

Re-enter the Old Town by this massive city gate. Its studded wooden door dates from the 18th century.
Turn left uphill to Plazuela de la Rogativa. Take the ramp on the right into the gardens. Paths cut up to Casa Blanca on the right.

3 CASA BLANCA

The daughter and son-in-law of island founder Ponce de León built the original fortified house in 1521. It contains a small museum of island history.
Return through the gardens and walk on up to the grassy headland and El Morro.

4 SAN FELIPE DEL MORRO

This weather-beaten stone fortress guards the entrance to San Juan Bay. It rises sheer from the shore, with walls up to 20 feet thick in places, and holds a maze of ramps and tunnels, lofty lookouts and dungeons. There are great views of the bay and around to Fort San Cristóbal.
Walk back across the headland and bear left on Calle Norzagaray, past the Cuartel de Ballaja, old Spanish barracks. Turn left up the steps of the Plaza del Quinto Centario.

5 PLAZA DE SAN JOSÉ

A statue of Ponce de León stands on the square, but the real sight here is the Iglesia de San José, a simple 16th-century church with a lavish altarpiece and monument to

Ponce de León statue in Plaza de San José

Ponce de León. Adjacent, the rickety Pablo Casals Museum displays cellos belonging to the famous musician.
Head a short distance west on Calle San Sebastián and look for the entrance to the narrow street of steps on the left.

6 ESCALINATAS

These attractive old streets made up of flights of steps are lined with beautifully restored pastel-painted town houses.
Turn left at the bottom of the first stepped street, right down the next step street, and left again at the bottom. Rejoin Calle Cristo by the 19th-century Cathedral and turn right. Continue along Calle Cristo.

7 CAPILLA DEL CRISTO

At the bottom of Calle Cristo, this tiny 18th-century chapel celebrates the miraculous escape of a horseman saved by divine intervention as he was set to plunge off the cliff. The chapel's gilded carvings, ornate silver altar, and oil paintings are revealed on Tuesday, Wednesday and Friday, 10.30am–3:30pm.

Casa Blanca museum – open: Tuesday to Sunday, 9am–noon and 1–4pm. Admission charge.
San Felipe del Morro – open: daily, 9:15am–6pm. Admission charge.
Pablo Casals Museum – open: Tuesday to Saturday, 9:30am–5:30pm; Sunday, 1–5pm. Free.

St. Kitt's and Nevis

*T*his brace of volcanic Leewards islands is separated by a 2-mile-wide channel known as The Narrows. St. Kitt's is the larger of the two (at 68 square miles), and is shaped like a tadpole, with the capital, Basseterre, on the southwest coast near the tail. A coast road circles the mountainous interior, dominated by Mount Liamuiga (3,792 feet/1,156m), while another road runs down the tail, flanked on either side by white-sand beaches.

The islands were sighted by Columbus in 1493, and he named the smaller one Nuestra Señora de las Nieves (Our Lady of the Snows) after its cloud-covered volcanic cone, which reminded him of a snow-capped peak. The larger island was christened St. Christopher after Columbus' own patron saint, and the patron saint of travelers. In time, both names were shortened to their present forms.

In 1623, St. Kitt's was the first Caribbean island to be colonized by the English. And in 1626, in a rare display of common European purpose, English and French settlers massacred the Carib population at Bloody Point, a few miles west of Basseterre. Otherwise, the two colonialist powers fought intermittently for control of the islands' lucrative sugar industry, until Britain gained the upper hand in 1783. St. Kitt's and Nevis achieved independence in 1983.

> **RAWLINS PLANTATION**
> Set in quiet countryside in the north of the island, this delectable plantation house hotel is a fine, quiet lunch stop. On the grounds, the Plantation Picture House exhibits Kate Spencer's watercolors. Tel: (869) 465 6221.

BASSETERRE

The pint-sized capital of St. Kitt's stretches back from the wharf between the twin poles of The Circus and Independence Square. Plumb in the center of The Circus, a Victorian clocktower serves as a public meeting place, surrounded by colonial buildings, with stone ground floors topped by wooden upper stories and laced with gingerbread detail. Chickens strut around grassy Independence Square, which is overlooked by the Catholic

ST. KITT'S

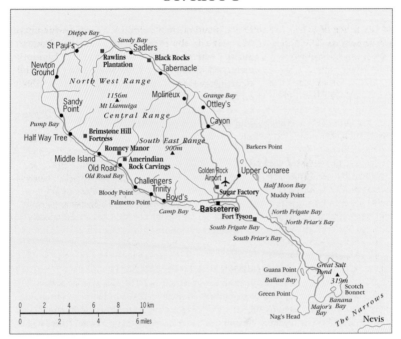

Church and Georgian houses. For a glimpse of old-time Basseterre, browse through the photographs at the St. Christopher Heritage Society, on Bank Street (free).

BRIMSTONE HILL FORTRESS

Founded by the British in 1690, this colossal 37-acre fortress crowns an 800-foot peak. Once known as the "Gibraltar of the West Indies," it was considered impregnable until 8,000 French troops managed to breach the 7-foot-thick Magazine Bastion walls after a month-long siege in 1782.

Cannons point out to sea from the battlements of Brimstone Hill fortress

Main Road, Brimstone Hill. Tel: (869) 465 2609. Open: daily, 9:30am–5:30pm. Admission charge.

ROMNEY MANOR

This modest, 17th-century great house is now home to Caribelle Batik, one of the island's most successful cottage industries. On the drive up to the house, a stone boulder features ancient Carib petroglyphs.
Tel: (869) 465 6253. Open: Monday to Friday, 8am–4pm. Free.

St. Kitt's and Nevis Department of Tourism – Pelican Mall, Basseterre, St. Kitt's. Tel: (869) 465 4040.

Nevis

The "Queen of the Caribbees," Nevis (pronounced *Nee-vis*) was one of the most prosperous islands in the Caribbean during the 17th and 18th centuries. Carpeted in cane fields and studded with elegant plantation houses (see box), it grew rich on its slave market and developed into a regular social whirligig, welcoming the likes of Horatio Nelson, who married local Frances (Fanny) Nesbit in 1787. *Allow 2 hours.*

1 CHARLESTOWN

The engagingly low-key island capital (population 1,500) sports a riot of gingerbread decoration, a few craft shops, and the interesting Alexander Hamilton House and Museum of Nevis History. This was the birthplace of 18th-century American statesman Alexander Hamilton, whose portrait graces U.S. $10 bills.

2 ST. JOHN'S FIG TREE CHURCH

Founded in 1680, and rebuilt in 1838, this pretty country church displays the wedding certificate of Horatio Nelson and Fanny Nisbet. (The couple were married on the Montpelier estate). You can see the memorial plaque Fanny erected to her parents on the right of the altar, and old tombstones concealed beneath the carpet in the aisle.

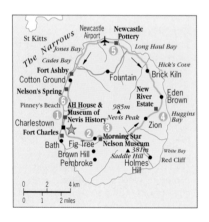

3 MORNING STAR NELSON MUSEUM

This small museum on the old Morning Star sugar plantation contains a wealth of fascinating Nelson memorabilia.

Alexander Hamilton House and Museum of Nevis History – open: Monday to Friday, 9am–4pm; Saturday, 9am–1pm. Admission charge.

Morning Star Nelson Museum – open: Monday to Friday, 9am–4pm; Saturday, 9am–1pm. Admission charge.

St. John's Fig Tree Church, where Nelson married Fanny Nesbit

There are scale models of Nelson's flagship HMS *Victory* and Nelson's Column, commemorative plates and snuff boxes, Staffordshire pottery figurines and paintings.

4 NEW RIVER ESTATE

Sugar production began at the 582-acre New River plantation in the 17th century and continued right up until 1956. You can stroll around the mill ruins, slowly disappearing beneath the undergrowth.

5 NEWCASTLE POTTERY

Just past the Nisbet Plantation (now a very nice hotel), this roadside pottery workshop turns out simple handmade jugs, plant pots, candle shades, and bowls, decorated with bird and lizard figures, made from local red clay.

PLANTER'S PARADISE

Many of the stately country houses built by rich Nevis sugar planters have been transformed into elegant hotels. If you feel like lunching in style, here are three suggestions:

Golden Rock Hotel: tables on patio terrace; tropical forest setting with walking trails. Tel: (869) 469 3346.

The Hermitage Inn: lovely antique-filled 18th-century house with terrace dining; gardens dotted with ginger-bread cottages. Tel: (869) 469 3477.

Montpelier Plantation Inn: very exclusive, beautifully restored stone house in lovely gardens. Tel: (869) 469 3462, reservations advisable.

---

6 PINNEY'S BEACH

The Fort Ashby ruins signal the northern extent of Pinney's Beach, which continues south in a sweep of golden sand, all the way to Charlestown. You can stop at St. Thomas Anglican Church, founded in 1643, and believed to be the oldest congregation on Nevis. From here, there are fine views along the coast. Take a look around the memorials decorating the interior. One such glowing epitaph commemorates 14-year-old Elizabeth Lake, "A Pious, Vertuous, Blamelesse, Spottlesse maid," who died in 1664.

A quiet road in Charlestown, the sleepy capital of Nevis

St. Lucia

St. Lucia (pronounced "*Loo-sha*") is one of the lushest and loveliest of all the Caribbean islands, with rich fertile plains and perfect sheltered harbors. This did not escape the notice of the British and French, who fought almost continually over the island between 1674 and 1814. During this period, St. Lucia changed hands no less than fourteen times. The decisive battle was a bloody affair at Morne Fortune in 1796, though it was another 18 years before the French finally ceded St. Lucia to the British. The island stayed under the Union Jack until independence in 1979, but a certain Gallic influence still remains.

Arriving by sea is the best way to view St. Lucia's famous Pitons, twin volcanic peaks that rise to a height of 2,400 feet sheer out of the sea. The modern cruise ship terminal, Pointe Seraphine, is a pleasant place to shop, but St. Lucia's capital, Castries, is of little interest. The best day-trip options are to head north for the beaches and Pigeon Island; or take a tour of the south, covered in the St. Lucia Drive (see pages 120–1).

CASTRIES

For a flourish of local color, Central Market, on Jeremie Street, is the best bet. Under cover you'll find straw hats and crafts, brooms made from palm fronds, and food stands selling huge slabs of cake and coconut turnovers. Outside, a profusion of fresh fruit and vegetables spills out onto the sidewalk. The other main sight in town is the Cathedral of the Immaculate Conception, on Derek Wallcot Square. Its interior is painted from floor to ceiling with biblical murals.

MORNE FORTUNE

The jungle-green hill of Morne Fortune (Hill of Good Luck) climbs up behind Castries, dotted with houses and hotels. At the peak, in the grounds of 18th-century Fort Charlotte, the Inniskillen Memorial commemorates the British fusiliers who captured the hill from the French in 1796. Farther down, Caribelle Batik demonstrate the ancient art of batik textile printing in their workshops.

PIGEON ISLAND NATIONAL HISTORIC PARK

Pigeon Island has a colorful history – former pirate lookout, 18th-century British naval headquarters, quarantine post, and turn-of-the-century whaling station. It is a great place to spend a lazy day on the beach. Or, for spectacular views south to the Pitons and north to Martinique, clamber up to the ruins of Fort Rodney (named after the famous British admiral who defeated the French fleet). There is a well-laid-out interpretation center in the old Officers' Mess, a waterfront café, and a botanical trail around Flamboyant trees, palms, yuccas, tamarinds, and scented frangipani.

Gros Islet, northwest coast. Open: daily, 9am–5pm; guided tours at 9:30am, 11:30am, and 2:30pm. Admission charge.

St. Lucia Tourist Board – PO Box 221, Pointe Seraphine, Castries. Tel: (758) 450 0603.

ST. LUCIA

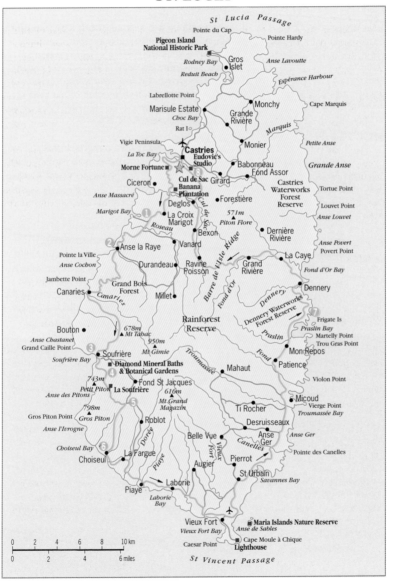

St Lucia Passage

Pointe du Cap

Pointe Hardy

Pigeon Island National Historic Park

Rodney Bay

Gros Islet

Anse Lavoutte

Reduit Beach

Espérance Harbour

Labrellotte Point

Monchy

Cape Marquis

Marisule Estate

Grande Rivière

Choc Bay

Rat I○

Marquis

Vigie Peninsula

Castries
Eudovic's Studio

Monier

Petite Anse

La Toc Bay

Morne Fortuné ■

Babonneau
Fond Assor

Grande Anse

Ciceron ●

Cul de Sac
Banana Plantation

Girard

Castries Waterworks Forest Reserve

Tortue Point

Anse Massacré

Deglos

Forestière

Louvet Point

Marigot Bay

La Croix
Marigot

571m ▲ Piton Flore

Anse Louvet

Roseau

Bexon

Dernière Rivière

Anse Povert

Vanard

Povert Point

Anse la Raye

La Caye

Pointe la Ville

Durandeau

Ravine Poisson

Grand Rivière

Fond d'Or Bay

Anse Cochon

Jambette Point

Grand Bois Forest

Dennery

Canaries ●

Canaries

Millet ●

Dennery Waterworks Forest Reserve

Frigate Is

Rainforest Reserve

Praslin

Praslin Bay

Bouton ●

678m ▲ Mt Tabac

Martelly Point

Anse Chastanet

950m ▲ Mt Gimie

Trou Gras Point

Grand Caille Point

Soufrière

Troumassée

Mon Repos

Soufrière Bay

Diamond Mineral Baths & Botanical Gardens

Patience

743m ▲ Petit Piton

Mahaut

Violon Point

Anse des Pitons

La Soufrière

Fond St Jacques

616m ▲ Mt Grand Magazin

Micoud

Vierge Point

798m ▲ Gros Piton

Gros Piton Point

Roblot

Ti Rocher

Troumassée Bay

Anse l'Ivrogne

Desruisseaux

Belle Vue

Anse Ger

Anse Ger

Choiseul Bay

La Fargue

Piaye

Augier

Pointe des Canelles

Choiseul

Pierrot

Dorée

St Urbain

Vieux Fort

Laborie

Savannes Bay

Piaye

Laborie Bay

Vieux Fort

Vieux Fort Bay

Maria Islands Nature Reserve

Anse de Sables

Caesar Point

■ Cape Moule à Chique
Lighthouse

St Vincent Passage

```
0    2    4    6    8    10 km
0    2    4    6 miles
```

St. Lucia

This drive down the west coast takes in beautiful bays and gardens, pretty fishing villages, and what claims to be the "world's only drive-in volcano" (see map on page 119). *You can cover most of this drive in a few hours, but to complete the circuit of the southern portion of the island, allow around 5 hours.*

1 MARIGOT BAY

Pretty as a picture, this bay has starred in several movies. (Rex Harrison's *Dr. Dolittle* once talked to the animals here). Today, the idyllic sheltered harbor, encircled by steep forested slopes, plays host to a busy marina and resort.

2 ANSE LA RAYE

Anse La Raye (it means Bay of the Rays – stingrays in this case) is a typical St. Lucian fishing village of little wooden cottages, rusty tin roofs, and splashes of aquamarine paint. The once plentiful rays have long since gone, but the fishermen are still here amidst piles of nets and examples of local boat building (hollowed out gomier trees) on the beachfront. In the village itself, check out the murals decorating the church and playground walls; also the La Sikwe Sugar Mill, on the edge of town.

Marigot Bay

3 SOUFRIÈRE TOWN AND THE PITONS

Though the famous Pitons (named for the French for "peaks") lie south of Soufrière, some of the best views can be enjoyed from the road as it runs down into town. A wander around Soufrière's main square will reveal the church, some gracious but rather tired old buildings laced with intricate, faded gingerbread decoration, and maybe the local ice-cream seller pedaling her or his cart and ringing a bell.

Drive to within a few hundred yards of La Soufrière's steaming, sulphurous pits

4 DIAMOND MINERAL BATHS AND BOTANICAL GARDENS

Bring your swimsuit if you want a cure in these mineral baths, once enjoyed by Louis XVI's troops. The warm, milky-grey waters are fed by an underground spring from the Soufrière volcano. Rather more attractive are the luxuriant botanical gardens and waterfalls where the rockface and riverbed have been dyed orange by mineral deposits.

5 LA SOUFRIÈRE

You can drive most of the way up to La Soufrière's sinister and very smelly sulphur springs; then walk the final few yards to the bubbling pits. Guides point out the various colored mineral deposits (green is copper oxide, purple is magnesium, and so on) and add some color of their own in the form of facts, figures, and gruesome stories.

At this point, you can return to Castries, or continue on around the southern coast.

6 CHOISEUL ARTS AND CRAFTS CENTER

A marvelous place to buy unusual craft souvenirs, the Center teaches young St. Lucians skills, such as wood carving, pottery, and weaving, and many develop into first-class artists. Visit the workshops, as well as the showroom.
Follow the coast road to Fregate Island.

7 FREGATE ISLAND

A good place for a leg stretch on the road back to Castries, this observation point overlooks the frigate bird nesting grounds just off the coast. The nesting season is from May to July, when the great birds (with a wingspan of over 6 feet) can be seen coming and going.
Continue north to Dennery; then head west on the cross-island road that runs through the banana plantations back to Castries.

8 EUDOVIC'S STUDIO

Vincent Eudovic, a former teacher at the Choiseul Crafts Center, is one of St. Lucia's most important artists, and his wood carvings are sold throughout the island. This is both his home and studio.
Return to Castries.

> **Botanical Gardens** – open: daily, 10am–5pm. Admission charge.
> **La Soufrière** – open: daily, 9am–5pm. Admission charge.

St. Martin/Sint Maarten

*T*his tiny island, with an area of just 37 square miles, is one of the most developed corners of the Caribbean. The French/Dutch division of the island dates from 1648. Local lore has it that a Frenchman and a Dutchman set off in different directions around the island, respectively armed with a bottle of brandy and a bottle of gin. The dividing line would be drawn between the point of their departure and where they met up. The Frenchman fared rather better, gaining a 21-square-mile portion of the island for La Belle France. The Dutch muttered darkly about wily French tactics (the strategic deployment of a nubile French maiden to delay their man), but accepted the lesser portion.

Despite this dual arrangement, the two halves of the island get along fine together. There are no internal border controls, and English is widely spoken throughout the island, as well as French and Dutch. Most cruise ships anchor off the Dutch capital of Philipsburg, an attractive shopper's paradise. If you plan on visiting both sides of the island, it is a good idea to head immediately for the French capital of Marigot and enjoy coffee and croissants on the harbor, before returning to the bustle of Philipsburg.

Breakfast of croissants and coffee in Marigot's sidewalk cafés

PHILIPSBURG

Philipsburg is the archetypal prettified West Indian town: its four main streets are intersected by *steegjes* (narrow alleys), painted in pastel colors, and adorned with gingerbread woodwork. Front Street is a 16-block, mile-long open-air shopping center, with a few fine old houses, such as the lovely Pasangghran Royal Inn, a 19th-century former governor's residence and the Sint Maarten Museum (No. 119). The museum's displays of buttons, bones, old musket balls, and other relics salvaged from HMS *Proselyte*, which sank in Grootbaai (Great Bay) in 1796, are of passing interest, but the century-old house is an attraction in itself.

Sint Maarten Museum. Open: Monday to Friday, 10am–4pm; Saturday, 10am–noon. Admission charge.

MARIGOT

Marigot is much more laid back than its Dutch counterpart, with sidewalk cafés, faded colonial buildings, and a colorful morning market on the waterfront. This is a great place to relax over a late breakfast and admire the harbor view, look around the French specialty stores, and maybe take a hike up to the 18th-century Fort St-Louis.

BEACHES

Both sides of the island boast good beaches, but the beaches on the French (topless) side are generally quieter with few facilities. The best is Baie Longue, on the west coast, with its neighbors, Plum Bay and Baie Rouge, close runners-up. Busy beaches with good facilities on the Dutch side include Mulletbaai (Mullet Bay), Simsonbaai (Simpson Bay), and Grootbaai (Great Beach) – the latter is within walking distance of Philipsburg via Front Street.

Sint Maarten Tourist Office – Imperial Building, W J Nisbeth Road 23, Philipsburg. Tel: (559–5) 22337; **St. Martin Office Municipale du Tourisme** – Marigot Waterfront. Tel: (590) 87.57.23.

The sandy beach is just a short walk from downtown Philipsburg's shops

ST. MARTIN/SINT MAARTEN

St. Vincent and the Grenadines

St. Vincent and the 45-mile trail of tiny Grenadine islands stretching down towards Grenada is a top spot for Caribbean yachters and other island hoppers. St. Vincent is the largest of the islands, at 133 square miles, often referred to as "the mainland" by the inhabitants of the 30 or so Grenadines, though many of these tiny cays are uninhabited.

St. Vincent is explosively fertile – they say you could plant a pencil here and it would grow. The impenetrable green jungle barrier of the mountainous interior kept the Europeans at bay for years, and it provided excellent cover for warring bands of "Yellow" (indigenous) and "Black" (descended from runaway slaves) Carib Indians. After the Carib Wars ended in 1797, the British finally took control of the island, where they grew sugarcane, arrowroot, and cotton.

St. Vincent and the Grenadines Tourist Office – Bay Street, Kingstown. Tel: (784) 457 1502.

KINGSTOWN

Behind the bustling waterfront, St. Vincent's capital leads back into the steep hills that enclose the harbor. On Tyrrell Street, the marzipan yellow-and-white St. George's Cathedral, contains a memorial to Major Alexander Leith, who put down the Carib Rebellion of 1795. Across the street, St. Mary's Catholic Cathedral is a bizarre neo-Gothic hodge-podge of black barley sugar columns, pinnacles, and turrets. Tyrrell Street runs out of town up to Fort Charlotte, with sweeping views to the Grenadines and inland to the island's volcanic vertebrae.

The former Curator's House in the Botanical Gardens is now a museum

ST. VINCENT AND THE GRENADINES

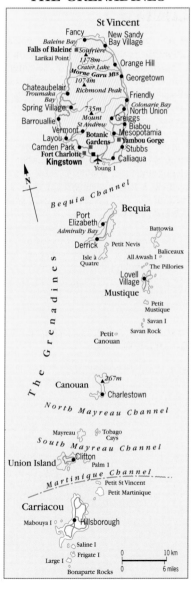

St. Vincent Botanic Gardens

Not to be missed, the oldest botanical gardens in the western hemisphere (founded 1765) contain an amazing variety of weird and wonderful flora. Tip a guide to show you the many oddities, such as the sealing wax palm, the cannonball tree, and the vast breadfruit tree, a descendant of the original tree bought to St. Vincent by Captain Bligh in 1793.
Open: daily, dawn to dusk. Free.

AROUND ST. VINCENT

Northeast of Kingstown, the fertile Mesopotamia Valley is a veritable market garden, growing bananas, breadfruit, coconuts, cocoa, nutmeg, arrowroot, and more. Day cruises head around the west coast to the lovely Falls of Baleine, which tumble 60 feet down from the slopes of La Soufrière, the landmark 4,049-foot, still-active volcano that dominates the northern sector of the island.

THE GRENADINES

Of the eight inhabited Grenadine islands, only two receive much in the way of visits from cruise ships. Just 8½ miles south of St. Vincent, stylish little Bequia (pronounced *Beck-way*) is fronted by Port Elizabeth on Admiralty Bay. Diversions include good craft and T-shirt shops, several pleasant waterfront eating places, and water taxis to the Princess Margaret and Lower Bay beaches. The island of Mayreau (pronounced *My-roo*) makes Bequia look like a teeming metropolis. There are two wonderful beaches. A steep hike up the hill to Dennis' Hideaway will enable you to admire the view with one of Capt. Dennis' lethal rum punches.

Tortola and the British Virgin Islands

*T*he Virgin Islands archipelago lies scattered across 1,000 square miles to the east of Puerto Rico. Less than a mile separates the westernmost British Virgin Island from its nearest U.S. cousin, St. John, but the dotted line on the map does more than divide British and U.S. territory. The boundary denotes a complete change of style. Tourism is relatively new in the 60-plus BVI (British Virgin Islands), of which only ten or so are populated. In fact, life is so laid back you have to search pretty hard for a pulse.

The first visitors were Arawak and Carib Indians, followed by Christopher Columbus in 1493. As he navigated the tricky channels around the archipelago, Columbus was so taken by the islands' beauty he named them after the 1,000 virgins in the legend of St. Ursula. After Sir Francis Drake sailed through the

VIRGIN ISLANDS

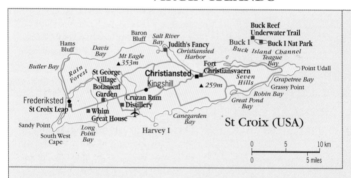

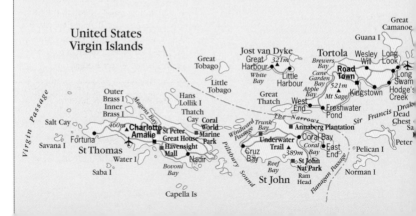

channel in 1585, pirates and buccaneers found the islands an ideal hideaway. British planters introduced slaves in the 18th century, but they had little success and sailed away, leaving the slaves behind. While other British islands sought independence in the 1960s, the BVI remained a Crown Colony. Economic ties with the USVI are strong (the U.S. dollar is local currency), but for the time being the inhabitants of the BVI are happy to remain separate and develop at their own (snail's) pace.

TORTOLA

The largest of the BVI (11 miles by 3 miles), Tortola's capital, Road Town,

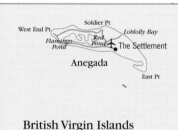

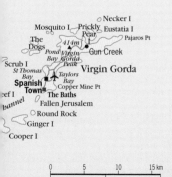

British Virgin Islands

sits on a fine bay in the lee of Sage Mountain. It is a small and unassuming place with a selection of craft and souvenir shops on Main Street, and a folk museum. The pretty J. R. O'Neal Botanic Gardens are worth a detour for their pergolas and palms, waterlily pond and bougainvillaea.

Taxis are readily available for short tours of the island. Top of the island's sights, quite literally, is Sage Mountain National Park, with fabulous views from the slopes of the 1,780-foot mountain, which is cloaked in primeval rainforest. Just north of here are lovely beaches at Cane Garden Bay and Apple Bay; while the marina and shopping complex at Soper's Hole, in the West End, makes a good break for lunch or a cool drink. *J. R. O'Neal Botanic Gardens. Open: Monday to Saturday, 9.30am–5.30pm; Sunday, noon–5pm. Admission by donation.*

VIRGIN GORDA

The "fat virgin" (so called because Colombus thought it looked like a pregnant woman reclining) was "re-discovered" by Laurance Rockefeller in the 1960s. He built a luxury resort here at Little Dix Bay, the first of several elegant, but low-key developments. Virgin Gorda also offers a selection of stunning coral-sand beaches, the best of which are in the southwest. Here, you'll find The Baths, a jumble of massive granite boulders embedded in the sand to form grottoes and caves at the water's edge.

Tortola/British Virgin Islands Tourist Board – Social Security Building, Waterfront Street, Road Town. Tel: (284) 494 3134.

Trinidad and Tobago

A twin-island state, Trinidad and Tobago are totally different. Trinidad is the larger of the two, at around 50 miles by 38 miles, and is the biggest of the Lesser Antilles islands. It is literally a chip off the block of South America, which occurred as recently as 10,000 years ago. Trinidad breaks from the traditional Caribbean island mold with an industrialized, oil-based economy and an unusually diverse multiracial population. Just 20 miles away, Tobago is much more like its Windward Island neighbors. This tranquil, Caribbean idyll, with its densely forested mountainous heart, combines fishing and farming with a more developed, though strictly low-key, tourist industry concentrated on its beautiful beaches (see pages 134–5).

The Arawak Indians' *Iere* (Land of the Hummingbird) was christened "Trinidad" (Trinity) by Columbus in 1498, after the three peaks that dominate its southern bay. A Spanish colony founded on the island in 1532 was destroyed (but not supplanted) by Sir Walter Raleigh in 1595, and thereafter the Spanish paid scant attention to Trinidad. French settlers introduced sugar and cocoa plantations towards the end of the 18th century, but Britain seized the island in 1797, and it was officially ceded to the Crown in 1802. With the abolition of slavery in 1834, African slaves deserted the plantations, and East Indian indentured laborers were shipped in to take their place. Between 1845 and 1917, some 145,000 Indians arrived in Trinidad, and many stayed on after their five-year term of labor. Indians and Africans now each account for approximately forty percent of the population. Chinese sugarcane field workers added further to the racial melting pot and, together with migrants from South America, Europe, and the Middle East, constitute the remaining twenty percent.

PORT OF SPAIN

The hectic Trinidadian capital is the island in microcosm, a welter of modern skyscrapers and West Indian gingerbread houses, pompous British colonial architecture, minarets, and mosques. On Frederick Street, the Indian markets and pavement stalls sell everything, from saris and bolts of Madras cotton to bootleg calypso tapes. Queen's Park Savannah is a huge, open, grassy breathing space with an eccentric collection of mansions nicknamed "The Magnificent Seven." North of here, the Botanical Gardens and Emperor Valley Zoo make an

Rastafarianism evolved in Jamaica, but is now widespread throughout the Caribbean

Queen's Royal College – one of the "Magnificent Seven," Port of Spain

excellent introduction to Trinidad's magnificent flora and fauna.
Botanical Gardens. Open: daily, dawn to dusk. Donations.

National Museum and Art Gallery
An informative overview of Trinidadian history and culture, the museum tells the island's story through historical exhibits, Amerindian artifacts, and artwork by leading local artists.
117 Frederick Street. Tel: (868) 623 5941. Open: Tuesday to Saturday, 10am–6pm. Free.

> **Trinidad & Tobago Tourism and Industrial Development Authority –** 10–14 Phillipps Street, Port of Spain. Tel: (868) 623 6022.

TRINIDAD

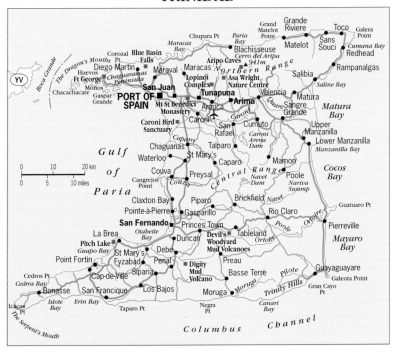

Palm-tree-fringed Maracas Bay boasts one of Trinidad's best beaches

CARONI BIRD SANCTUARY

This 450-acre marsh, mangrove, and lagoon sanctuary is home to the Trinidadian national bird, the scarlet ibis, as well as 149 other bird species, 80 types of fish, alligator-like caymans, sloths, and great carpets of waterlilies. Tours are made by flat-bottomed boats, and the highlight (if time allows) is the spectacular dusk flight of ibises.
8 miles south of Port of Spain.

CHAGUARAMAS PENINSULA

Leased to the American military during World War II, this peninsula is now protected as part of the Chaguaramas National Park. There is a clutch of islands just off the western end of the peninsula, one of which, Gasparee, boasts a cave complex adorned with stalactites and stalagmites. Another diversion is the Blue Basin Falls in the Diego Martin Valley (northern Chaguaramas Peninsula). It is a 10- to 15-minute walk from the parking lot to the freshwater pool and waterfall, which is recommended for a cooling dip.
Northwest of Port of Spain.

FORT GEORGE

This fortress-cum-signal station was built in 1804. Fort George lies an hour's drive to the west of Port of Spain. At 1,100 feet above sea level, it affords superb views over the island capital and across to the mountains of northern Venezuela.
10 miles west of Port of Spain.

MARACAS BAY

The road north from Port of Spain, known as Saddle Road or the "Skyline Highway," cuts a scenic roller-coaster

ASA WRIGHT NATURE CENTER

A must on any island tour, the Nature Center was established in 1967, at the Spring Hill Estate, on the edge of the rain forest. The old plantation house has been turned into a hotel, so nature lovers can actually stay up here and bird-watch from the balcony. Five trails lead off into the forest preserve, which plays host to a stunning variety of native hummingbirds, butterflies, toucans, and rare nocturnal oilbirds (or guacharos), once hunted by the Amerindians for their oil.
Near Arima, a 90-minute drive from Port of Spain. Tel: (868) 667 4655. Open: daily, 9am–5pm. Admission charge.

route through to the coast. There are superb views along the way, and the magnificent, palm-fringed, sandy beach at Maracas Bay is a popular spot on weekends, with changing facilities and refreshments.

18 miles north of Port of Spain.

PITCH LAKE

Worth a mention, though probably not practical for day trippers (it is a good six-hour round-trip from Port of Spain), this 90-acre asphalt "lake" is a truly bizarre natural phenomenon. It is said Sir Walter Raleigh caulked his ships with the black tar that seeps through the earth's crust and forms a bouncy skin that you can walk on. Around 300 feet deep at its center, the level of the lake is slowly dropping as it is mined for sale around the world.

In the southwest, near La Brea.

Trinidadian carnival goers spend months preparing their spectacular costumes

CARNIVAL

Introduced by French settlers during the 18th century, the Trinidad Carnival (or *Mas* – short for masquerade) is one of the biggest street parties in the world. Hundreds of thousands of Trinidadians and visitors, many of whom have crossed the world just to be here for Carnival, pack the streets of Port of Spain for the main competitions and parades, which start on the Friday before Ash Wednesday. The sea of glittering costumes, dancers and devils, bird-men and butterfly-women sashay and strut to the rhythms of steel bands and the strains of calypso banter from the "tents" (stages). It is an almighty but well-organized free-for-all with competitions galore, culminating in the Parade of Bands (Tuesday), which proceeds up Frederick Street to the Savannah.

ORIGINS OF CALYPSO

Music is the heartbeat of the Caribbean, and no other musical style has such wide currency in the region as calypso. Trinidad is the home of calypso, where it was first recorded in the 19th century, but it is now widespread throughout the islands.

Calypso's roots lie buried deep in the West African slave tradition of singing. Forbidden to speak in their native tongues, slaves were, however, allowed to sing. This chink in the planter's cruel "seasoning" process (see pages 102–3) was swiftly turned into a means of keeping African story-telling traditions alive. Many of the songs had an allegorical slant, using animals or birds to hide real identities. As such, they were protest songs and a way of passing on information or gossip. The very word "calypso" may be derived from the West African *kai-so*, an expression of encouragment or approval.

Protest, information, and gossip laced with humor are still the cornerstones of calypso today. The basic two-four or four-four rhythm does not permit an immense range of melodies, but calypso is strongly judged on its lyrical content, and its exponents are hailed as poet-

performers in the West African troubadour tradition. Calypsonians pull no punches. Their subject matter covers the spectrum, from love, life, and politics to cricket and baldly stated warnings about AIDS. Styles vary from belligerent to raucous, to downright raunchy. In competitions, other opponents are considered fair game and can be demolished with a few swipes of wickedly barbed humor.

The big names in calypso are partial to some pretty grandiose titles themselves: Lord Nelson and Lord Kitchener, King Pharoah and the Black Stalin amongst them.

The biggest of them all is the Mighty Sparrow. His career has spanned over 30 years, with more Roadmarch

Calypso has become a way of life

Below: The Mighty Sparrow – chief exponent of calypso

(the top Trinidad Carnival calypso award) titles to his name than any other.

Although calypso was largely a male preserve in its early days, many calypsonians are now women, who often adopt the title "Lady." The first woman to walk off with the Roadmarch title was Calypso Rose (Rose Lewis), in 1978. But don't expect the "Ladies" to stand on ceremony as their lyrics are every bit as provocative, witty, and hard-hitting as those of their male colleagues.

Tobago

*T*rinidad's little sister makes a virtue of being different. Tobago is smaller – but prettier. The sedate lifestyle is so much more relaxing – perfect for vacationers who want to unwind – and there is little crime. Whereas Trinidadians tend to write off Tobagonians as being a bit slow (though they still love to come here for weekend breaks), the people of Tobago pride themselves on being friendlier and more welcoming than the street-sharp "Trickidadians."

TOBAGO

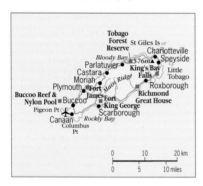

Beautiful Pigeon Point Beach

Trinidad and Tobago's political links originated fairly recently. A former pirate enclave turned prosperous sugar island, Tobago was grouped and governed with the Windward Islands until the late 19th century, when the sugar industry collapsed. The island went bankrupt and was appended to up-and-coming Trinidad. Poor and underdeveloped, relying on subsistence agriculture for much of this century, Tobago has been rescued by the emergent tourism industry, which is determinedly low-key. The island's chief charms include unspoiled tropical forests and excellent snorkeling.

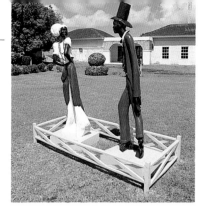

Contemporary art and sculpture find a home at historic Fort King George

SCARBOROUGH

A sleepy little split-level town with a small cruise ship complex, Scarborough is the island capital. Down near the harbor, there is a colorful market, and the Botanic Gardens are a short walk away. Farther uphill, remnants of the colonial era include the 1825 House of Assembly and Gun Bridge, with railings made from recycled rifle barrels.
Botanic Gardens – open: daily, dawn to dusk. Free.

Fort King George

Perched on the hilltop, 430 feet above town, this 18th-century British fortress makes a terrific lookout point, with views across to Trinidad. It now houses a fine arts center and gallery in the old officers' mess, as well as a small museum of Amerindian and colonial artifacts in the Barrack Guard House.
Open site. Free. Museum open: Monday to Friday, 9am–5pm. Free.

KING'S BAY FALLS

Hemmed in by the mountainous heights of the Main Ridge, King's Bay cuts into the southeastern corner of the island. The waterfalls are the highest in Tobago, with natural bathing pools and changing facilities. Guides are available for hikes to these and more distant falls.

PIGEON POINT

This is the classic Caribbean beach—a strand of powder-soft white sand fringed with palms. There are a snack bar, changing facilities, water sports, and glass-bottomed boat trips out to the superb Buccoo Reef National Park.
Open: daily. Admission charge.

TOBAGO FOREST RESERVE

Another favorite spot for nature lovers, the Tobago Forest Reserve is the oldest of its kind in the western hemisphere, set aside by the British in 1764. Near Bloody Bay Lookout Site, the Main Ridge Forest Trail begins its winding descent through the rain forest to Bloody Bay, named after a gory ancient battle when the sand and sea turned red with spilled blood. Tropical birds and large, brilliant butterflies dazzle beneath the forest canopy.
Set above the northwest coast, near Parlatuvier.

ROBINSON CRUSOE

Stop for a chat in Tobago, and it is almost certain you will be regaled with tales of the island's favorite character, the shipwrecked mariner namesake of Daniel Defoe's novel *Robinson Crusoe*. Published in 1719, Defoe's novel was based on the real-life exploits of one Alexander Selkirk, who was shipwrecked in the Pacific, off the coast of Chile. But Defoe employed a little artistic license to move his hero to Tobago. The Tobagans, in turn, have adopted Crusoe and even named a cave for him on the northwest coast.

U.S. Virgin Islands

The "American Paradise," the U.S. Virgin Islands are a collection of some 50 islands and cays east of Puerto Rico. The three main islands are St. Thomas and St. John, in the north, and St. Croix (pronounced *Croy*), out on a limb some 40 miles due south. Commercialism is all pervasive in St. Croix and St. Thomas, where the familiar trappings of fast food and hotel chains, shiny automobiles and cable TV make them two of the most developed islands in the Caribbean. St. John is an exception, since two-thirds of its 16 square miles is a protected national park. (See map on pages 126–7.)

The Steeple Building in Christiansted now houses the National Parks Museum

Christopher Columbus anchored off St. Croix on November 13, 1493, on his second voyage to the New World. The following day he set sail for the islands on the northern horizon and spent four days charting the jumble of islands he named *La Once Mil Virgenes* (the 11,000 Virgins). The Spanish tried to settle St. Croix shortly afterwards, but it was abandoned for over a century. Dutch, English, and French colonists arrived next in 1625, but were ousted by the Spanish in 1650, who in turn were almost immediately evicted by the French.

Meanwhile, the Danish West Indies Company set up a permanent base on St. Thomas in 1671, claimed St. John in 1684, and set to work planting sugarcane, cotton, and indigo estates. St. Croix was bought from the French in 1733. St. Thomas was declared a free port in 1724 and profited handsomely from the European conflicts being fought in the Caribbean. During the American War of Independence, Danish neutrality and St. Thomas' free port status initiated strong ties with the U.S. An early attempt by the U.S. to buy the islands from the Danes in 1867 was vetoed by the islanders, but in 1917, the collapse of the sugar trade finally persuaded the islands' inhabitants to opt for the U.S. bid.

ST. CROIX

The largest of the Virgin Islands (82.2 square miles), St. Croix has two cruise ship piers: Christiansted, the capital, accommodates smaller vessels; while big ships put in at Frederiksted, 17 miles west. Badly hit by Hurricane Hugo in 1989 (though most of the damage has now been repaired), "Croy" is far behind St. Thomas in the tourist development stakes, but this is part of its charm. There are fewer crowds and the locals have more time to chat.

CHRISTIANSTED

A delightful small port settlement set back from the harbor and toy-town Fort Christiansvaern, Christiansted offers good shopping and some great little restaurants and bars. The settlement was originally founded in 1733, and there are still several 18th- and 19th-century buildings dotted about. The most notable of these is the Steeple Building, a former Lutheran church that now houses a modest museum of local history.

Offshore to the east of Christiansted, the 850-acre Buck Island National Park offers the best beach on (or rather off) the island, as well as excellent snorkeling and diving with two underwater trails. Frequent boat services for the island leave from the docks in Christiansted.

Fort Christiansvaern

Bearing more than a passing resemblance to a rather large toy castle, this yellow-and-white fortress was largely completed

USVI/St Croix – PO Box 4538, 41A Queen Cross Street, Christiansted, 00822–4538 USVI. Tel: (340) 773 0495.
St. Thomas Tourism Division Visitors' Bureau – PO Box 6400, Charlotte Amalie, 00804 USVI. Tel: (340) 774 8784.

between 1738 and 1749. It has been restored to its appearance circa 1830–40, with neat green painted shutters and pyramids of cannon balls. On the upper story, a small historical exhibition traces the origins of the fort.
Tel: (809) 773 1460. Open: Monday to Friday, 9am–4pm. Admission charge (includes entrance to the Steeple Building museum).

Buck Island National Park is just a short boat ride from the dock at Christiansted

Yachts off Caneel Bay, on the northwest coast of St. John, U.S. Virgin Islands

CRUZAN RUM FACTORY

This is a favorite stop on the tourist trail in the western corner of the island. The modern factory was built on the grounds of the former Diamond Sugar Plantation, though today molasses, the raw ingredient for rum, has to be imported. Half-hour tours trace the distilling process, followed by tastings.
Off Centerline Road, near the airport. Tel: (340) 772 0799. Open: Monday to Friday, 9–11.30am, 1–4.15pm.

FREDERIKSTED

St. Croix's second town, Frederiksted runs along two streets from Fort Frederik. Pretty stone arcades, topped with gingerbread decoration, protect passersby from the sun's glare.

Fort Frederik

Blood-red Fort Frederik, which dates back to 1760, was destroyed by fire in 1878, and restored in Victorian style, and now houses a well-displayed and informative museum covering island history and culture, with a good section on hurricanes. In 1776, the new American flag received its first foreign salute from the cannons of Fort Frederik. Today, the 18th-century battlement weaponry lies silent.
Tel: (340) 772 2021. Open: Monday to Friday, 8:30am–4pm. Donation.

ST. CROIX LEAP

Here in St. Croix's mini "rain forest," craftspeople at the St. Croix LEAP (Life Experience Achievement Program) fashion all sorts of craft items from free-form sculptures to walking sticks and fridge magnets made from mahogany, saman, and thibet wood.
Mahogany Road, Route 76. Tel: (340) 772 0421.

ST. GEORGE VILLAGE BOTANICAL GARDEN

On a 16-acre site where Arawak Indians once set up camp and the Danes operated a sugar mill from 1733 to 1917, this botanical garden showcases over 800 species of tropical plants. A circuit of the gardens, which are attractively laid out amongst the ruins of the old plantation buildings, takes around 40 minutes. There is plenty to admire, including orchid and fern houses, a fragrant

Trunk Bay, St. John, is rated one of the top ten beaches in the world

frangipani walk, and a rain forest trail. *Centerline Road, near Frederiksted. Tel: (340) 772 3874. Open: Tuesday to Saturday, 9am–4pm. Admission charge.*

WHIM GREAT HOUSE AND MUSEUM

Don't miss this gracious 18th-century house with 3-foot-thick walls, and an air moat designed to keep the cellar cool. The unusual oval-shaped interior has been restored with period colonial furnishings and paintings. On the grounds, the sugar estate's old windmill and cane crushers can still be seen. *Centerline Road. Tel: (340) 772 0598. Open: guided tours Monday to Saturday, 10am–4pm. Admission charge.*

ST. JOHN

A short boat ride from St. Thomas, St. John is one of the best-preserved islands in the Caribbean. In 1956, two-thirds of the island was given by owner Laurance Rockefeller to the National Parks Service. Since then, the land-based portion of the 12,900-acre preserve has been returned to its natural forest state.

Around 5,600 acres of the park lie under water off the north coast. Most visitors to the island are day trippers; there are frequent daily sailings from Charlotte Amalie and Red Hook (St. Thomas) to Cruz Bay. The Visitors' Center near the Cruz Bay ferry dock has information about the park and its 22 walking trails, which range from 10 minutes to a couple of hours.

St. John's best beaches are in the north. Trunk Bay, rated among National Geographic's top ten beaches, has snack facilities, snorkel rental, and an underwater trail.

Admiring the view from the Estate Annaberg site, a former sugar plantation on St. John

Charlotte Amalie is one of the top shopping spots in the Caribbean

CHARLOTTE AMALIE

A pretty waterfront town clambering back into the hills from the mercantile mayhem on Main Street, Charlotte Amalie is a major cruise ship destination that services up to ten ships a day. The downtown area is a shrine to duty-free shopping, but if you prefer a breath of fresh air and a taste of the town's history, take a stroll up Government Hill to explore the quiet streets of 19th-century public buildings and hotels linked by flights of steps.

The most famous flight is the "99 Steps," which lead up to the commanding lookout point known as Blackbeard's Tower. Local legend claims the ferocious pirate maintained a base on the island in the 1690s and early 1700s. His days of lacing rum with gun powder and splicing his beard with burning charges before going into battle ended when his ship, the *Queen Anne's Revenge*, was captured by Lieutenant Robert Maynard of the British navy in 1718, and Blackbeard was killed in the fight. There are also several possible excursions beyond the capital.

ST. THOMAS

When Dutch planters and the Danish West India Company first set up shop on St. Thomas in the 1670s, the harbor settlement outside the walls of Fort Christian was known as *Taphus*, literally "tap house," a welcome watering hole for Caribbean merchants. *Taphus* was rechristened "Charlotte Amalie" in 1691, in honor of the Danish queen. Before long, the dockside warehouses were piled high with goods from around the world, a tradition that has continued right through to the present day – though the contents are now Japanese electronics, French perfumes, and designer fashions rather than rum, guns, indigo, and cotton.

ATLANTIS SUBMARINES

This is a great way to appreciate the wonders and surprises of the marine world along the 1½-mile stretch of Buck Island Reef, without getting wet. The hugely popular Atlantis Submarine dives reach a depth of 90 feet beneath the surface, and experienced divers keep up a running commentary during the dive. *Open: daily, with frequent departures hourly from Havensight Mall. Reservations necessary; booking ahead through the cruise line is recommended. Tel: (340) 776 5650.*

Colonial chic: the Legislature of the U.S. Virgin Islands, Charlotte Amalie

CORAL WORLD MARINE PARK AND UNDERWATER OBSERVATORY

An alternative introduction to the marine world, this small but effective complex features an 80,000-gallon reef tank, "predator" tanks, a touch tank, and a walk-in observatory. Check out the fish feeding schedules for additional action. The park also offers changing facilities and showers for visitors who want to relax on neighboring Coki Beach.

Northeast coast. Tel: (340) 775 1555. Open: daily, 9am–5pm (6pm in winter). Admission charge.

ESTATE ST. PETER GREAT HOUSE AND BOTANICAL GARDENS

The outstanding feature of this contemporary great house are its fabulous views. From the observation deck at 1,000 feet above sea level, you can see twenty other islands. Take a stroll around the gardens, where more than 500 varieties of plants flourish, and

tour the exhibition of local artists' work.

St. Peter Mount Road. Tel: (340) 774 4999. Open: daily, 9am–4pm. Admission charge.

MAGENS BAY

This fabulous beach boasts over a mile of talcum-powder sand sandwiched between serried ranks of palm trees and limpid blue water. It features in National Geographic's list of top ten beaches in the world (along with Trunk Bay, on St. John).

North coast.

The Frederick Evangelical Lutheran Church, on Government Hill

THE ORIGINS OF CARNIVAL

The explosion of color, music, song and dance that is the Caribbean carnival actually has its roots in medieval Europe. The very word "carnival" is derived from the Italian *carnevale*, which means the removal of meat, and refers to the Christian practice of Lenten abstinence in the period before Easter. Carnival was brought to the New World by Europeans, notably the Spanish and the French Catholic planters who decamped to Trinidad as revolutionary unrest hit the French possessions at the end of the 18th century.

Between Christmas and Ash Wednesday, the French settlers indulged in a hectic season of parties and masked balls, or *masquerades*, which, shortened to *Mas,* is still a commonly used Trinidadian term for carnival. With Emancipation in 1838, and the lifting of laws prohibiting slave gatherings and drumming, the former slaves celebrated their freedom every August with processions, took to the streets for fun at Christmas, and before long hijacked the pre-Lenten Mardi Gras. The result was a fusion of West African and European traditions in which folklore performances partnered stilt-riding mocko-jumbies (make-believe spirits) with characters straight out of Biblical tales, and stately quadrilles or waltzes were revamped to an African beat. The emergence of calypso in the 19th century, and steel bands in the 1940s (thanks to the oil drums abandoned by the U.S. military after World War II), set a truly Caribbean seal on the event.

Trinidad is still the home of Caribbean carnival (see page 131), but every island has its own version of Carnival. Some, like Bahamanian Junkanoo, are held over the Christmas period, while July and August see the Cropover (harvest) and Emancipation carnivals on many islands.

Drums and elaborate costumes are essential ingredients of the carnival scene

GETTING AWAY FROM IT ALL

"*Every one of the islands has, for me, its own special scent . . . . islands like Grenada or St. Vincent float in a subtle aroma of spices.*"
DANE CHANDOS,
Isles to Windward, 1955

Getting Away from It All

Nature lovers will have a wonderful vacation in the Caribbean, where finding a quiet area of outstanding natural beauty is (as they say in these parts) "no problem." That goes for Southern Florida, too, home of the Everglades National Park and its 2,000-plus different plant species. After all, Juan Ponce de León named the land *La Florida* after the Spanish Eastertide Festival of Flowers.

There are more than 200 varieties of colorful hibiscus in the Caribbean region

Since the days of the early explorers, visitors to the Caribbean region have never ceased to be amazed and delighted by the beauty and diversity of the islands. Beneath cool, green rain forest canopies, in cottage window boxes and botanic gardens, even along the roadside, colorful plants and flowers grow in luxuriant profusion. Caribbean land animals are quite limited by comparison. Iguanas, some of which can grow up to 5-feet long, and a couple of rare lizards are about the most exciting things to see. And there are several types of inordinately loud tree frog, such as the Puerto Rican *coqui*, named for its mating call (apparently, the "ko" sound attracts the females and the "kee" warns off the males).

Everybody enjoys the flutter and zing of giant butterflies and tiny humming-birds, as they flit from bloom to bloom, and bird-watchers are definitely in for a treat in this neck of the woods. Ornithological types will find themselves reaching repeatedly for their binoculars in the hope of spotting a rare parrot or some of the other brightly plumed indigenous island species. Rain forest preserves offer superb bird-watching opportunities, as do swamp and marshlands like the Black River in Jamaica, and the Caroni Swamp in Trinidad, where the evening flight of the scarlet ibis at Caroni is one of the natural wonders of the world.

Most Caribbean islands boast nature reserves and national park areas, but on-site facilities vary tremendously from country to country. In more developed islands, parks may offer visitor centers with interpretive displays, helpful literature, marked trails, and guided walk programs. However, this is not always the case, and you are strongly advised not to set off into wilderness areas without an experienced local guide.

Neither does nature stop at the shoreline in the Caribbean. What better

The magnificent frigate bird, or man-o'-war, with a wingspan measuring up to 7 feet

way to escape the crowds than spend a couple of hours snorkeling among delicate coral reefs? There are snorkeling opportunities off most of the islands, where the only crowds come in shoals, and the underwater landscape is stunningly beautiful. Areas such as the Caymans and Dutch ABC islands offer some of the most spectacular diving in the world.

MIAMI AND FORT LAUDERDALE

Allow a full day to visit the Everglades National Park from Miami or Fort Lauderdale (see pages 40–1). The Main Entrance and Park Information Center (tel: (305) 242 7700; open: daily, 8am–5pm) lie 10 miles southwest of Florida City. The Information Center shows an introductory film and provides brochures, maps, and details of boat tours, canoe rentals, and guided walks that depart from the Royal Palm Interpretive Center. The northern entrance to the park is at Shark Valley, 35 miles west of downtown Miami, via the Tamiami Trail (US41). The Information Center (tel: (305) 221 8776; open: daily, 8:30am–5.15pm) can advise on trails, bicycle rental, and tram tours.

ANTIGUA

For some of the island's finest and least-frequented beaches, head for the southwest corner of Antigua. Just offshore, Cades Reef is an excellent dive site. Nearby Fig Tree Drive climbs up through Antigua's last remaining patch of lush, undeveloped forest.

ARUBA

Getting away from it all in Aruba could be an equestrian foray into the *cunucu*, as they call the back country here, or a gallop along the sands on horseback.

Both novice and experienced riders are welcome to join guided horseback tours from Rancho El Paso, Washington 44 (tel: (297) 873310). Bird-watchers can find peace and quiet at Bubali Pond, an old salt pan now set aside as a sanctuary north of Oranjestad, near Noord.

The exotic lobster claw flower pops up in Caribbean gardens and on flower stalls

Dominica's lush rain forest quickly swallows up paths and trails

BAHAMAS

Nassau's Botanical Gardens offer a cat's cradle of paths, steps, and leafy bowers, grafted onto the hillside below Fort Charlotte. On Grand Bahama, the 100-acre Rand Memorial Nature Center boasts twenty-one species of wild orchids, nature trails, an aviary, and forest ecology exhibits.

Botanical Gardens – open: daily, 8am–4pm. Admission charge.

Rand Memorial Nature Center – open: Monday to Friday, 9am–4pm (guided walks at 10am and 2pm). Admission charge.

BARBADOS

Start out at Hackleton's Cliff, a magnificent viewpoint 1,000 feet above the windward coast on St. Joseph, and descend the path through Joe's River Tropical Rain Forest to the ocean. The 85-acre woodland preserve is renowned for its giant ficus trees, stands of mahogany, cabbage palms, and bearded fig trees (banyans), which give the island its name. On seeing the banyans' muddle of aerial roots growing down from their branches, Portugese sailors called the island *Los Barbudos*, "the bearded ones."

BERMUDA

Once upon a time, visitors to Bermuda would have been able to "rattle and shake" from one end of the island to the other by rail. Taken out of service 30 years ago, the old railroad has been given a new lease on life as the Bermuda Railway Trail. Pick up a free guide to the trail from the tourist office. It is broken up into easy-to-walk sections of around 2 miles each, and there is access from numerous points around the island.

BONAIRE

Bonaire is famous for its flamingos. There are two colonies on the island. The smaller one is in the north at Goto

Meer. The Pekel Meer bird sanctuary in the southern salt pan is also home to many of Bonaire's other 124 bird species. Washington Slagbaai National Park occupies a former plantation site in the northern part of the island and features hiking trails, caves, and a representative collection of hardy native plants, such as cacti and windswept divi-divi trees.

CAYMAN ISLANDS

Opened by its regal namesake in 1994, the Queen Elizabeth II Botanic Park features a well-marked woodland trail, swamp area, iguana habitat, and ponds for freshwater turtles, as well as over 200 plant species. Keen bird-watchers can enjoy the Governor Michael Gore Bird Sanctuary, a 3½-acre wetland preserve.

CURAÇAO

The 4,500-acre Christoffel National Park was created from three old plantations in the northwestern corner of the island. It harbors native deer, iguanas, and rare lizards, as well as many of Curaçao's 500 different species of plants and flowers. Within the park, four short trails for walkers and cars scale the sides of the

Christoffelberg, Curaçao's highest hill, at 1,239 feet.

DOMINICA

On the western slopes of Mount Diablotin, the Northern Forest Reserve is an important refuge for two endangered parrot species. The 20-inch tall Sisserou (imperial parrot) is one of the largest Amazon parrots, with mainly green plumage and deep purple breast feathers; its more colorful cousin, the Jaco (red-necked parrot), is distinguished by a tell-tale flash of scarlet at its throat.

GRENADA

La Sagesse Nature Center is a former private estate in an isolated spot on the south coast. It combines woodland trails, areas of scrub cactus, and mangrove estuary with three lovely beaches and offshore coral reefs. On the north coast, the beautiful Levera National Park area offers trails, beaches, and snorkeling. It's busy on weekends, but virtually deserted during the week.

Wild flamingos acquire their coloring from eating shellfish, notably shrimp

Crocodiles can be difficult to spot as they nose log-like around the shallows

GUADELOUPE

Some 480 miles of marked trails wend their way around the 75,000-acre Parc Naturel on Basse-Terre. The Maison du Parc on the Route de la Traversée is a good starting point for excursions into the rain forest (see page 88). One trail makes an exciting crossing of the Bras David River via a wooden suspension bridge.

JAMAICA

Jamaica is a natural wonderland with marvelous bird life. The national bird is the doctor bird, or red-billed streamertail, a busy-body little emerald-colored hummingbird that zips around local gardens. Jamaica boasts more than 250 species of bird, about 25 of which are endemic. A strange but true story: The hero of Jamaican resident Ian Fleming's best-selling books was named after the author of *Birds of the West Indies*, James Bond.

A great place to learn about Jamaican bird life is the Rocklands Bird Feeding Station at Anchovy, within easy reach of Montego Bay (see page 94). At Black River, in the southwest of the island, 90-minute boat rides explore the mangrove swamp area known as the Great Morass. An expert guide points out birds, basking crocodiles, and other wildlife. Black River Safaris depart daily: 9am, 11am, 12.30pm, 2pm, and 4pm. On the road south, stop off to visit the lovely YS Falls. These unspoiled cascades and pools are some of the most beautiful on the island. Bring a swimsuit.

MARTINIQUE

North of Le Morne Rouge, near the little village of Ajoupa-Bouillon, is the narrow ravine of the Gorges de la Falaise, carved from the volcanic flank of Mt. Pelée by the Falaise River. During the winter months, you can walk up the riverbed to a set of falls. Nearby at Les Ombrages,

Safari boats explore Jamaica's Black River and "Great Morass" swamp

there is a shady botanical trail through a well-watered ravine fed by springs and waterfalls, plus a *boo kai*, or traditional Martiniquan kitchen garden.

PUERTO RICO

It rains 350 days a year on Puerto Rico's El Yunque Caribbean Rain Forest, but for nature lovers this is one of the most spectacular sights in the Caribbean (see page 111). A variety of trails set out from the Visitors' Center following gushing mountain streams past explosions of bromeliads, hibiscus, and stalks of bamboo over 200 feet high.

ST. CROIX

St. Croix's 15-acre patch of semi-rain forest lies east of Frederiksted, bisected by the Mahogany Road. Trails and vehicle tracks criss-cross beneath 100-foot-tall mahogany trees, surrounded by lush ferns and invaded by bromeliads.

ST. JOHN/ST. THOMAS

The St. John National Park is one of the natural treasures of the Caribbean. Rent a jeep, strike out on foot, or join a guided walk from the National Park Service headquarters in Cruz Bay. Horseback tours can be made with Cardina Stables, Coral Bay (tel: (340) 693 5161). A highlight is the Estate Annaberg plantation ruin on the central north coast.

ST. KITT'S

It is a full day trip to Mount Liamuiga crater lake, set in St. Kitt's highest peak (3,792 feet/1,156m). The paths are not

easy to follow without a guide, but it's definitely worth the effort. Shorter trips can also be made into the rain forest. Kriss Tours (tel: (869) 465 4042) can arrange full- and half-day guided hiking tours. For something less strenuous, Nevis Equestrian Center (tel: (869) 469 3106) offers horseback tours in the mountains and beach gallops.

Bathers can enjoy the unspoiled cascades and pools of the YS Falls, Jamaica

RAIN FOREST

The rain forest is the richest type of habitat on the surface of the earth, a veritable treasury of plant and animal life. Just 4 square miles of rain forest may contain up to 750 species of trees, 1,000-plus varieties of smaller flowering plants, 400 species of birds, 125 types of mammals, and 150 different butterflies and moths. All it asks in return is an annual rainfall in excess of 70 inches and relatively high temperatures with little seasonal variation.

When Columbus first arrived in the Caribbean, almost every island was covered in primeval rain forest. But within a few hundred years, European settlers cleared vast tracts for their plantations, leaving the flatter islands, such as Antigua, virtually barren. Mountainous islands, such as the Windwards, Jamaica, and Puerto Rico, were more fortunate, since their inaccessible volcanic uplands proved

(air plants) are nonparasitic and survive by gathering water

and nutrients, which run down the bark.

Visiting the rain forest is a wonderful experience, but it is recommended that you take a guide if venturing off the beaten track. As well as providing a fund of anecdotes, local guides can spot the "unseen" – from a rare parrot to tree frog tadpoles swimming in a bromeliad water reservoir. Hikers should dress sensibly in sturdy boots and loose-fitting cotton clothes. Improbable as it may seem when you are down by the beach, it can get quite chilly at higher altitudes, so take a light sweater or jacket if you are heading for the mountains.

more than a match for the plunderous sugar barons.

The Caribbean rain forest is not as well-stocked with wildlife as, say, the Amazon, but it is still fascinating. The framework of the forest is provided by mahogany, gommier, and other massive trees that grow over 100 feet tall, forming a dense canopy. In the cool gloom below, lianas (climbing plants) scramble up towards the light, and the vast green cavern is festooned with ferns, mosses, orchids, and bromeliads growing out of tree trunks and branches. Although they are attached to a host, these epiphytes

Top left: view over the rain forest
Above: Guadeloupe's National Park
Opposite page – far left: giant ferns
Left: the exotic "ginger" plant

St. Lucia's twin volcanic peaks, the Pitons, rise from the sea on the west coast

ST. LUCIA

East of Soufrière, the rain forest backbone of St. Lucia offers some lovely walks and fine views back to the Pitons. North of Castries, the Forestry Division maintains the short Union Nature Trail together with a mini-zoo and an herb garden. Call ahead (tel: (758) 450 2231).

ST. MARTIN/SINT MAARTEN

It is not easy to get away from it all on this tiny island, but the northwestern corner is markedly less developed, and there are a few footpaths for determined explorers.

ST. THOMAS

See St. John, page 149.

ST. VINCENT

The best hike on St. Vincent is the three-hour trek up Soufrière, but with limited time the tropical forest trails down the Buccament Valley (northwest of Kingstown) are more accessible. This is good bird-watching territory, and you may even spot the rare St. Vincent parrot.

TORTOLA

The Sage Mountain National Park offers two interesting diversions off the main trail. One cuts through semi-rain forest, while the other leads via a 20-year-old mahogany plantation to a lookout at 1,710 feet above sea level – the highest point in the Virgin Islands.

TRINIDAD AND TOBAGO

Trinidad's spectacular bird life and flora are legendary. The island boasts around 425 species of birds (both permanent residents and winter visitors), plus over 2,200 different species of flowering plants and trees. The best place to enjoy an overview of this is the Asa Wright Nature Centre (see page 130). If time permits, be sure to catch the dusk return of the scarlet ibis from the feeding grounds to their roosts in the Caroni Swamp (see page 130). For details of the Tobago Forest Reserve, see page 135.

Blooming marvelous: Brilliant Caribbean flora attracts the birds and butterflies

DIRECTORY

"The time has come," the Walrus said,
"To talk of many things:
Of shoes – and ships – and sealing wax -
Of cabbages – and kings –"
LEWIS CARROLL,
Alice Through the Looking-Glass, from 1871

Shopping

*F*or many holiday makers, shopping in new and exotic locations rates as their single most popular holiday pursuit. This will come as no surprise to the storekeepers of the Caribbean, who welcome the souvenir-hungry tide of visiting shopaholics with open arms and some notable bargains. Several Caribbean cruise destinations, such as St. Thomas and St. Martin, are duty-free ports offering the promise of twenty-five to fifty percent savings against U.S. prices on some luxury goods. However, it pays to know the prices back home before splashing out. On other islands, duty-free stores, often conveniently located right by the cruise ship pier, do a roaring trade in luxury items, such as Japanese cameras, jewelry, and French perfumes. For something with a touch more local flavor, check out boutiques selling Caribbean-style fashions in lovely bright cotton designs, or trawl the numerous galleries exhibiting local arts and crafts. Exuberant Caribbean markets are fun to explore. Piled high with exotic fruits, strange vegetables, pots, pans, and fast food stalls, they are a great place to pick up straw hats and mats, beach bags and fragrant packages of dried spices.

Key West's Mallory Market

MIAMI

A water-taxi service from the Port of Miami ferries passengers to Bayside Marketplace, a top Miami shopping attraction (see page 23), and there are services to Miami Beach, where top shopping spots include the Lincoln Road Mall, the galleries and antiques stores of Española Way (see page 31), and the classy Bal Harbour Mall. The Coconut Grove district offers dozens of individual stores and two mini malls; while Coral Gables' Miracle Mile is worth a visit.

FORT LAUDERDALE

The stylish boutiques and fashionable galleries of Las Olas Boulevard are the sophisticated shopper's first port of call in Fort Lauderdale. In the department store field, Nieman Marcus, Saks Fifth Avenue, and Lord & Taylor gather in the Galleria Mall on E Sunrise Boulevard, near the beach. Two other major

The world's top vacation pastime, shopping is a firm favorite with cruise ship passengers

shopping, dining and entertainment complexes are Las Olas Riverfront, and the vast Beach Place Mall, on AIA, offering a mix of well-known brand-name fashion stores and individual boutiques. Bargain hunters should head west to Sawgrass Mills, on W Sunrise Boulevard. This is claimed to be the world's largest discount mall, with over 200 manufacturer and retail outlets.

KEY WEST

Key West's main drag, Duval Street, is a magnet for shoppers. T-shirts, beach and resort wear, and all manner of crafts are featured here. For great deals on T-shirts, slip off to the T-Shirt Factory, 316 Simonton Street, which offers outlet prices and multipurchase discounts. Just up the street, Key West Handprint Fabrics, 201 Simonton Street, produces a colorful range of cool cotton casual wear and table and furniture coverings.

ANTIGUA

Fresh off the ship, cruise passengers have to run the gauntlet of the modern Heritage Quay duty-free complex before reaching the streets of St. Johns. If you're looking for shopping with character, head instead for neighboring Redcliffe Quay, housed in attractively restored wooden buildings. Look out for contemporary jewelry in The Goldsmitty; comfortable Caribbean-made cotton leisure wear in the sparsely elegant BASE store; jaunty nautical style casual clothes in Windjammer Clothing; and Kate Spencer's gorgeous painted silk creations and vibrant Caribbean prints in Kate Designs.

ARUBA

A short step from the pier, Seaport Village offers an international collection of fashion stores, jewelry, and other duty-free items. Several local stores specialize in typically Dutch souvenirs, such as tiny porcelain gabled houses straight off the canals of Amsterdam, mini-windmills, and Delft tiles. Look, too, on Caya G F Betico Croes, where Gandelman Jewelers stocks an extensive range of clocks and watches, and the Aruba Trading Company is a duty-free treasure trove.

Stalls in Nassau's popular Straw Market spill out onto Bay Street

BAHAMAS

The islands' major shopping complex, Freeport/Lucaya's International Bazaar and Straw Market on Grand Bahama Island is pretty overwhelming to all but the most dedicated shopaholics. Store prices vary from around 20 to 30 percent below U.S. retail prices, while bargaining is expected in the Straw Market. Another favorite shopper's haunt is the attractively laid out Port Lucaya shopping and dining complex. Shopping in New Providence is centered on Nassau's Bay Street, an eight-block strip of duty-free stores, T-shirt shops, and a Straw Market. Prices are similar to those in Grand Bahama and vary little from shop to shop.

BARBADOS

The Bridgetown Harbor cruise ship complex and downtown Broad Street offer the widest choice of duty-free shopping in a range of boutiques and department stores. In Holetown, the Chattel House Village is an attractive shopping complex where the Cave Shepherd department store leads the duty-free field. The Best of Barbados craft chain has several shops around the island, including one at Andromeda Gardens. They carry top-quality local crafts and a range of gifts, from hot sauce and Caribbean cook books to flower and plant guides.

BERMUDA

Tax-free Bermuda is an excellent place to stock up on life's little luxuries. The British influence is obvious in the tweeds and cashmere, the fine china and Edinburgh crystal. On Front Street, Hamilton, the three leading department stores are A S Cooper, H A & E Smith's, and Trimingham's. Fellow bastions of impeccable taste include Archie Brown & Son (woolens), Crisson's (jewelry), and William Bluck and Company (china and

Souvenir T-shirts are big sellers, but prices vary little from shop to shop

Local crafts run the gamut, from straw hats to oil paintings and wood carvings

glass). All the main stores have outposts in St. George, and there are several pleasant shops in the Somers Wharf complex here. The Royal Naval Dockyard has an understandable leaning towards nautical-type gifts and memorabilia, as well as antiques.

CAYMAN ISLANDS
Grand Cayman is a free port and British Crown Colony, so Scottish woolens, Irish linen, crystal, and bone china are favorite buys. Most of the shopping action takes place on Fort Street and Cardinal Avenue around the Kirk Freeport Plaza. South of George Town, on South Church Street, Pure Art displays a tempting array of island crafts in a Cayman cottage. (NB. Black coral and turtle products cannot be imported into many countries, including the U.S. and U.K.)

CURAÇAO
Willemstad's Breedestraat, Heerenstraat, and Madurostraat are renowned for the quality and variety of their numerous stores. Swiss watches, French perfumes, Italian fashions, leather goods, linen, and liquor abound. Spritzer & Fuhrmann, the top Dutch jeweler on Gomezplein, also sells a good range of china and crystal. Penha & Sons, Heerenstraat 1, fills the oldest building in town with other luxury temptations. For lovely linen, try New Amsterdam, Gomezplein 14.

DOMINICA
Carib baskets and wood sculptures are the traditional souvenirs from Dominica. In

Dominica's Carib Indians preserve traditional basket-weaving skills

Roseau, Tropicrafts (on the corner of Queen Mary Street and Turkey Lane) stocks a large selection of woven baskets in traditional three-tone (white, brown and cream) designs. They also sell wooden parrot carvings, costume dolls, and gift baskets containing bay rum, coconut oil soaps, and spices. Another good place to find souvenirs is the Papillote Wilderness Retreat gift shop, near Trafalgar Falls.

GRENADA
Don't leave Grenada without a handful of sweet-smelling spices or without browsing through the local handicrafts. In St. George's, a handful of gift shops on Cross and Young Streets stock attractive batik items, basketwork, jewelry, and carvings. Yellow Poui Art Gallery, at Young Street and The Esplanades is the place to find local and Caribbean art, antique maps, and prints. There are also several craft shops on The Carenage.

GUADELOUPE

The Centre St-John Perse shopping complex by the cruise terminal contains a stylish French mix of souvenir and clothing stores, perfumeries and stylish little pharmacies stocking toiletries concocted from provençal herbs. Some stores offer a 20 percent discount for purchases made with credit cards or travelers checks. For more boutique shopping, head for rue Schoelcher and rue Frébault. For atmosphere and spices, don't miss the noisy Covered Market.

Traditional costumed dolls dressed in bright Madras cotton on sale in Guadeloupe

JAMAICA

Some of the best Jamaican souvenirs are edible or drinkable, such as Blue Mountain coffee, rum, and the coffee liqueur, Tia Maria. The island is also well-known for its colorful tropical print fabrics transformed into attractive casual wear, and for its handicrafts – from jauntily painted carved animals and fish to pottery. The best of Jamaican crafts are on display at Harmony Hall, just outside Ocho Rios. The Gallery of West Indian Art, 1 Orange Lane, Montego Bay, concentrates on

contemporary Jamaican and Haitian paintings, but also has a small but tasteful selection of craft items. For serious shopping in town, avoid the high-pressure touristy "craft markets," and make for the air-conditioned comfort of shopping malls, such as Coconut Grove or Island Plaza in Ocho Rios, and the City Center Mall and Half Moon Village in Montego Bay.

MARTINIQUE

Stretching west off rue de la Liberté and the Savane to rue de la République, Fort-de-France's main shopping district is crammed into a grid of narrow streets, bristling with French brand names. Chanel, Baccarat, Guerlain, Lalique, and others are all here, and some stores offer a 20 percent discounts on items paid for by credit card or travelers check. The jewelry stores around rue Lamartine/rue Isambert are the place to find Creole gold knot necklaces and "slave chains," which make unusual souvenirs. Handicraft items are on sale at the Centre des Métiers d'Art in the Savane gardens; and Martiniquan rum is some of the best in the Caribbean.

PUERTO RICO

Calle Fortaleza and Calle San Francisco run the length of Old San Juan, forming two seamless stretches of T-shirt and jewelry stores, fashion boutiques, craft shops, and galleries. It is a browser's paradise, with another tempting selection of shops on Calle Cristo, where the Ralph Lauren (Polo) Factory Outlet discounts casual wear. The Centro de Artes Populares, in the Convento de los Dominicos, Plaza de San José, offers a full range of Puerto Rican crafts, leather wear, jewelry, wood and stone carvings, hammocks, and pottery, including *santos*, little clay religious figures and Christmas cribs. For a terrific selection of Haitian art and folk crafts, check out the Haitian Gallery, 387 Calle Fortaleza (east end).

ST. BARTHÉLEMY

As befits a duty-free port, Gustavia's shops carry a good selection of luxury items, such as watches, liquor, perfumes, china, and glass, but bargains are few and far between. The only local handicraft of note is basket weaving. In addition to sun hats and bags, bread baskets are a specialty.

Popular buys: Caribbean wood carvings display a distinct African influence

ST. CROIX

The best shopping is in Christiansted, around Strandgade and Kongensgade. Folk Art Traders, on Strandgade, stocks a wealth of colorful Caribbean crafts and some rather more unusual items, such as jewelry made from larimar (a semiprecious sky-blue stone); amber from the Dominican Republic; genuine "pieces of eight" (old Spanish coins); pottery from Puerto Rico; and lignum vitae wood carvings and Haitian

paintings. The options are rather more limited in Frederiksted, though you'll find several craft and souvenir shops on waterfront Strand Street. The Whim Great House and Museum has a good gift shop. Another favorite souvenir is a bottle of St. Croix's own high-quality Cruzan rum.

Roadside craft stall, Jamaica

Local craft shops are not only picturesque but can offer bargain buys

ST. KITT'S

Gifts, clothing, and duty-free items are all available from the waterfront Pelican Mall complex; while up on The Circus, Island Hoppers sells pretty printed cottons, hand-painted pottery and wooden decorations, plus Caribelle batiks. For the biggest choice of Caribelle's popular cotton fashions and wall hangings, take a trip to the factory and shop at Romney Manor (see page 115).

ST. LUCIA

The attractive new Pointe Seraphine duty-free complex, right by the cruise ship pier, offers one-stop shopping for everything from a little black frock to a helicopter tour of the island. Bagshaw Studios has a branch here, selling their colorful, printed cotton designs featuring parrots, seahorses, hibiscus, and other animal and jungle-type motifs; but it is more fun to visit their studio and shop at La Toc. For crafts buys, check out the Market and Noah's Arkade on Jeremie Street.

ST. MARTIN/SINT MAARTEN

Front Street, Philipsburg, is a duty-free shopping haven with great deals on all sorts of luxury items, such as jewelry, watches, fine wines, and leather. The Shipwreck Shop is a good place to find colorful local crafts, Caribelle batik clothes and beach wraps, and jewelry. Front Street also features several galleries. Guavaberry liqueurs are an island specialty, on sale at the Guavaberry Kiosk (No. 10). On the French side of the island, Marigot has its fair share of chic boutiques and Gallic goodies.

ST. THOMAS

Shopping in downtown Charlotte Amalie is not recommended for the faint-hearted. Over 400 shops are crammed into the area between Main Street and the waterfront, and they are packed with every conceivable luxury and souvenir item. Cruise passengers berthing at Havensite will find another fully fledged mall at the bottom of the gangplank. St. Thomas' tax-free status results in savings of around 20 percent on U.S. prices. For shopping at a less frenetic pace, Tillet Gardens, near Tutu, is a delightful artisans' enclave with galleries, crafts studios, a restaurant, and pet iguanas lounging under the trees.

Craft shops in historic buildings on Road Town's main street, Tortola (BVI)

Street stands greet cruise passengers on the Philipsburg waterfront, Sint Maarten

ST. VINCENT AND THE GRENADINES

Shopping is a very low-key affair in Kingstown. Artisans Local Art and Craft, upstairs in the Bonadie Building on Bay Street, sells basketware and scented mats made from plaited lavender, Straw art, and hand-painted clothing. Noah's Arkade, Bay Street, stocks Caribbean souvenirs. Voyager, Halifax Street, stocks duty-free items. Bequia offers more choice, with a selection of beach-style boutiques selling silkscreen *pareos* (brightly colored cotton wraparound skirts) and swimwear. Local Colour has some great T-shirts with unusual Caribbean designs, a small selection of sterling silver jewelry, artsy cards, and island prints. Along the waterfront, local craftspeople sell model boats, and tie-dyed shorts and vests.

TORTOLA

Road Town's shops are cosily accommodated in little wooden houses on Main Street and include the art work, crafts and the foodie temptations of Sunny Caribbee (guava jelly, spicy chutneys, and wooden pots of West Indian Hangover Cure), as well as Pussers – purveyors of yachting clothing,

scrimshaw, rum, and other nautical regalia.

TRINIDAD AND TOBAGO

Frederick Street, in Port of Spain, is one huge international bazaar. Here, you will find everything from Swiss watches, Swedish silver, and French brandy to Indian saris, carnival costumes, and calypso tapes. For luxury items, check out Stecher's (No. 27); for more basic shopping requirements, just duck into the Indian bazaars and fabric shops at the southern end of the street.

Tobago greets cruise ship visitors with a harborside mall at Scarborough. On Bacolet Street, The Cotton House Studio does a good line in tie-dye and batik fashions and jewelry.

Caribbean artisans keep craft traditions alive thanks to tourist dollars

Entertainment

*A*mong the most hotly discussed topics on any cruise is the standard and variety of the onboard entertainment. Most large cruise ships offer a day-long program that kicks off after breakfast with activities, from aerobics on the pool deck to mid-morning bingo. There may be a steel band to accompany lunch, a pianist tinkling the ivories at cocktail time, and an after-dinner show. Night owls who are still raring to go can gamble into the wee small hours, or disport themselves in the disco. How the cruise director manages to summon up a smile and a quip after organizing all this remains one of the great mysteries of our time.

Obviously, the type and extent of on-board entertainment varies considerably from ship to ship. A small cruise ship cannot possibly have the facilities available to a larger vessel. It cannot, for instance, even accommodate flocks of dancers for Las Vegas-type show productions, let alone stage them. The passenger profile also has a bearing on the content of the entertainment program. "Party ships" do not offer ballroom dancing or bridge lessons; cruise lines catering to a more sedate crowd will not go in for cocktail drinking competitions or limbo dancing.

When choosing a cruise, it is helpful to know what the cruise company offers in the way of entertainment. What good is a laser disco if you like to dance in the old-fashioned way? Children may be enchanted by Disney characters at breakfast, but chances are the adults won't. Is the swimming pool big enough for you? Check out if there is a formal evening, too, as you may want to pack a suit or dress. The problem with much of the onboard entertainment is that it can appear a bit bland. But considering the cruise company's near impossible task of pleasing most of the people most of the time, perhaps this is inevitable.

Limbo dancing is perhaps best left to professional local cabaret performers

Good sports: pillow fighting on a slippery pole slung over the pool

Bars, lounges, and showrooms

The ship's bar (or bars) is very definitely the focus of social life on board. The main bar may feature a pianist or a cabaret act in the evening to accompany cocktail hour or to entertain those people who are sitting out the main show. There is also usually a pool bar for drinks on deck. Except on luxury "all-inclusive" ships, drinks must be paid for in cash or charged to passengers' accounts. If they are signed for (keep receipts), a total bill will be presented at the end of the cruise. Prices are similar to those charged at a resort – not cheap.

If the bar has been declared an "entertainment-free zone," then the evening pianist-cum-cabaret act may perform in a lounge with its own bar. During the day, lounges may be used for port talks (usually a brief history and lots of shopping information covering the next port of call), bingo and trivia games, or any other indoor group activity.

The main lounge is often referred to as the showroom or theater. With a stage, lighting rig, and theater-style seating arrangements, this is the scene of the evening show that can vary in content from an all-singing, all-dancing sparkly costumed production to a variety evening featuring magicians, jugglers, and comedians. This is the time when members of the cruise entertainments staff pop up to do a short turn of their own. There are usually two shows per evening, or the same show twice, playing for the first and second dinner seatings.

Cabaret time at the Palladium Showlounge aboard Celebrity Cruises' *Horizon*

There is plenty of opportunity for on-deck games, such as shuffleboard

CASINOS
Casinos are always closed in port due to customs regulations, but once a cruise ship sails into international waters the cards are shuffled, the slot machines jangle into life, and the serious business of onboard gambling gets underway. It is big business for the cruise lines, and several of them operate "cruises to nowhere," aimed specifically at gambling addicts. Many ships offer a "full casino" with baccarat, blackjack, craps, poker, and roulette, as well as the usual slot machines.

DISCOTHÈQUES AND DANCING
Hardly a cruise ship puts to sea without a dance floor, but facilities vary considerably. All mainstream cruise ships have discothèques with a resident DJ, who supposedly gears musical selections to customers. Mostly this is modern disco-dance music, but sometimes a Big Band or Swingtime evening might lure older passengers onto the dance floor. On some "party ships"

the sound system, light show, and special effects are good enough to bear comparison with the best land-based discothèques and nightclubs. Some ships also have a low-key nightclub where you can just about talk over the music, or dance to a band.

EXERCISE FACILITIES
It is a fact that the average passenger gains around four pounds over the duration of a week-long cruise. To redress this unhealthy situation, cruise companies usually provide a choice of exercise opportunities. Health and fitness facilities on a larger cruise vessel may run the gamut, from a gym and weight room to a sauna and solarium. Some even include a jogging track. The fitness director will organize aerobics or stretch classes for groups of various fitness levels, and advise on other physical activities. The upper deck is generally the place to find outdoor games, such as badminton, shuffleboard, volleyball, and the like. On the pool deck, bathing facilities can range

from the sublime (waterslides or whirl pools) to the faintly ridiculous (postage stamp-sized pools crossed in three strokes).

GAME ROOMS AND LIBRARIES

For passengers who enjoy a gentle rubber of bridge or a nail-biting game of Risk, most ships provide a game room with card tables and a selection of board games. The library often doubles up as a venue for card players to meet, so a rowdy game of snap is probably not in order. Friendly tournaments can be arranged by the entertainments staff, and a small prize may be offered.

Shipboard libraries are not usually very extensive. There might be a modest selection of periodicals, best-seller paperbacks, classics, and reference books covering flora, fauna, and other information about the region.

MOVIE THEATERS

A cruise can be a good way of catching up on the latest movies. As many as half a dozen or more films will be shown on a regular basis during a week-long cruise. Details will be listed on the daily activities program.

Some modern ships, or those that have been recently refurbished, have televisions and/or VCRs in their cabins. There is normally a movie channel and satellite reception of U.S. and other programs, plus a video library.

SHORE EXCURSIONS

This is supposed to be "sightseeing made easy," but independent-minded passengers may feel short-changed by these all-too-brief forays. Most shore excursions depart in a convoy of coaches from the pier, accompanied by a local guide. Many only last for a couple of hours, so passengers wanting lunch on board can be back in time, thus the time spent at the various attractions is severely curtailed.

Trained instructors and fully equipped exercise rooms help passengers keep fit

Children

*O*nce upon a time, a child on a cruise ship was the proverbial lonely little petunia in an onion patch. The odd nanny-supervised tea party and a three-legged race around the deck was considered "entertainment." The rest of the time a child's role was to be rarely seen and absolutely never heard. Now, all that has changed, and junior cruisers have never had it so good.

In recent years, cruise companies have grabbed a significant slice of the family vacation market by offering a raft of tempting fare deals, special facilities, and the promise of a safe and easily supervised environment. Most ships provide some form of organized children's program, while others are exclusively family-orientated. When booking a family cruise vacation, it is important to find out not only what the cruise company offers in the way of activities, but also what age group they are aimed at.

Activity programs

These can vary tremendously in content and in the frequency with which they are offered. Some ships only run children's

programs on days when the ship is at sea, or during the school holidays. Child-orientated cruise lines, such as Disney Cruise Line, offer a full daily program of events for children and teenagers of all ages, year-round. Activities progams can incorporate anything from dressing up as pirates for a pool party to computer programing. Arts and crafts classes, quizzes and magic shows may also be on offer. Most cruise lines provide a supervised children's play area, and there may be swimming and sports instruction, too. Some of the best and most broad-ranging children's programs are offered by Carnival Cruise Line, Celebrity Cruises and Norwegian Cruise Line. Premier Cruise Lines to the Bahamas offer tie-ins with several Florida theme parks and sail with a full complement of Looney Tunes characters on board.

Babies

There is no reason the baby should not come too, but parents are advised to make a few inquiries first. With adequate advance warning (at the time of booking), cruise lines will provide cots, high chairs, and other baby and toddler paraphernalia. Check if baby food and formula are available on board. Again, advance warning will do the trick, but

Children love cruising in the Caribbean and make new friends easily

Enjoying the Dolphin Experience, run by the Underwater Explorers Society, Lucaya

diapers are generally not part of the service. Parents traveling with small children, or those who like dinner without the kids every now and then, should check the availability of baby-sitters in advance. Some ships provide a pool of sitters for both day and night duty, either for free or for a small hourly rate. On non-child orientated vessels, parents may have to make arrangements with a sympathetic staff member or parents in a similar position.

Kids Cuisine
Parents of fussy eaters will do well to check out children's catering arrangements ahead of time. Most children would trade all the gourmet delicacies in the world for a simple hamburger and fries, and many of the more child-friendly cruise lines recognize this by providing special children's menus. As a rule, families with young children will be given the early dinner sitting (around 6:30pm or 7pm).

SUN ALERT
Everybody should take care in the hot Caribbean sun, but children are particularly susceptible to its burning rays. Make sure they are well-covered with a high-factor sunscreen every morning before going out to play. Apply it throughout the day, and try and make them wear a hat.

Sports

*W*ater sports, quite obviously, is the name of the game in the Caribbean. But there is plenty for landlubbers too: fishing, hiking, golf, cycling, tennis, and horseback riding are all usually offered. Local tourist offices and their overseas branches have details of most sports facilities and special sporting events.

Bike paths in Florida offer some novel hazards for cyclists

(certified) divers will have no problem finding dive operators offering trips on most Caribbean islands. The local tourist office will have a list. Snorkelers can paddle about off any beach to their heart's content.

The best dive sites in the Caribbean are found off the Bahamas, Grand Cayman, and Dutch Leeward Islands. On Grand Bahama, UNEXSO (tel: (242) 373 1244) offers 10 to 12 trips daily for experienced divers, and an excellent short instruction course for beginners. Bob de Soto's Diving Ltd. (tel: (345) 949 2022) is a top operator in Grand Cayman. Try De Palm Watersports in Aruba (tel: (297) 824400) and Curaçao Seascape in Curaçao (tel: (599) 4625905 ext 177). Curaçao Underwater Park (tel: (599) 4624242) is a snorkeler's paradise, with easy-to-follow trails.

Dive enthusiasts in Florida should contact: Diver's Paradise, Key Biscayne, Miami (tel: (305) 361 3483); Pro-Dive, Fort Lauderdale (tel: (305) 761 3413); and, for access to the Looe Key National Marine Sanctuary (30 miles north of Key West), try Looe Key Dive Center, Ramrod Key (tel: (305) 872 2215). Another superb Keys dive site and possible day trip from Miami, is the John Pennekamp Coral Reef State Park on Key Largo (tel: (305) 451 1621).

CYCLING

On weekends, the French islands of Martinique and Guadeloupe are a blur of lycra-clad cyclists tearing up and down swooping mountain roads. Mountain bikes (called VTT in French, pronounced *vay-tay-tay*) can be rented for the day or by the hour on many islands.

DIVING AND SNORKELING

Some specialist cruise vessels, such as the Windstar and Sea Goddess ships, are fully equipped with scuba and snorkeling gear, while others may offer snorkeling as a shore excursion option. Experienced

The Caribbean islands and Florida Keys offer some of the finest diving in the world

GOLF

Golf is an increasingly popular pastime in the Caribbean, and there are courses springing up all over the place. Many are attached to resort complexes, but most welcome visitors and can arrange equipment rental, instruction, and caddies. During the busy winter season, it is advisable to make arrangments in advance, but even a last-minute inquiry may be successful, as cruise-ship timing often means playing during the hottest part of the day.

Grand Bahama has three of the best courses in the Caribbean: Bahamas Princess (tel: (242) 352 6721); Fortune Hills Golf and Country Club (tel: (242) 373 4500); and Lucayan Golf & Country Club (tel: (242) 373 1066). Other recommended courses include Bermuda's challenging Trent Jones-designed Port Royal Golf Course(tel: (441) 234 0974); Golf de l'Imperatrice

Joséphine at Les Trois-Ilets, Martinique (tel: (596) 68.32.81); and the Carambola Golf Course in St. Croix (tel: (340) 778 5638). For sheer scenery, it would be hard to beat Mahogany Run in St. Thomas (tel: (340) 777 6006).

Florida is a golfer's paradise. There are dozens of courses in the Greater Miami and Greater Fort Lauderdale areas. Contact the relevant Visitors and Convention Bureau for a golfing guide.

Golfers can enjoy the facilities at several beautiful Caribbean courses

HIKING AND WALKING

Ecotourism is a growth industry in the islands as an increasing number of visitors quit the crowded beaches in search of the "real Caribbean." Rain forest trails, mountain lakes, and volcanic craters provide a wealth of stupendous scenery and a great opportunity to stretch your legs. Local guiding companies have sprung up all over the place, and their services are recommended for anybody keen to step off the beaten track. Without knowledgeable local expert, it is easy to get lost. Paths and trails can disappear with alarming speed, washed away by floods or simply reclaimed by

the undergrowth. Day-long hikes are often impractical for cruise passengers, as they tend to start at dawn in the coolest time of day, long before the cruise ships have lowered their gangplanks. But it is still possible to get away from it all on shorter trails and in the many national parks. Tourist offices can provide lists of guides (you may want to contact them in advance), and often carry information and maps covering short island walks or historic walks around town. Always dress comfortably for hiking. Sturdy shoes and loose-fitting cotton clothes are recommended. Always take a hat and plenty of water.

Screaming reels: sportfishers strike it
lucky in Atlantic waters

HORSEBACK RIDING

Riding is a great way to explore off the
beaten track, and local tourist offices will
have a list of stables offering guided treks
in the countryside or on the beach. Check
whether the stable supplies hard hats.

SPORTFISHING

Most Caribbean marinas harbor a sport
fishing operator or two. There is no
mistaking those elevated lookout towers
and the selection of whippy-looking rods
lined up on stern designed to lure passing
anglers aboard. Deep-sea fishing for
wahoo, tuna, marlin, mahi-mahi (also
known as "dolphin" – not to be confused
with the friendly mammal of the same
name), and the magnificent sailfish is
available off most of the islands. One of
the hottest spots for the fishing fraternity
is Grand Cayman, which also reckons to
have the best bonefishing in the world and
devotes the month of June to the Million
Dollar Month Fishing Tournament.
There are over a dozen deep-sea fishing
charter operators offering full- and half-
day charters, all equipment supplied.
They include Charter Boat Headquarters
(tel: (345) 945 4340) and Crosby Ebanks
(tel: (345) 945 4049).

Florida is also a big-time sportfishing
center. Fort Lauderdale's Bahia Mar
Yacht Center is full of gleaming charter
fishing boats. Or head north to Pompano
Beach (7 miles), the modestly titled
"Swordfish Capital of the World," where
the Hillsnoro Inlet Charter Fleet (tel:
(954) 943 8222) operates a dozen vessels.
The Florida Keys are a magnet for keen
anglers with time to spare on the
mainland. Every marina has its sport-
fishing charter boats, and barely a month

goes by without a big money fishing
tournament run out of Islamorada (Sport
Fishing Capital of the World) in the
Middle Keys.

TENNIS

It is not usually easy for cruise ship
passengers to find a tennis court, as most
of them are attached to hotels and
reserved for the use of guests. However,
check with the local tourist office for news
of friendly resorts or rare public courts.
Hotels may insist on players wearing
whites on court.

Big blue: windsurfing off the Bahamas

WATER SPORTS

As a rule of thumb, wherever there are
beachfront hotels there are bound to be
water sports facilities. In major resort
areas, waterskiing, jet skiing, and para-
sailing (the practice of being hauled
high in the air behind a fast-moving boat
while attached to a parachute) are all part
of the fun. Windsurfers, pedalboats,
Hobie Cats, Sunfish, and other small
sailing boats are also widely available for
rental through hotels or independent
water sports outfits. Yachting is a favorite
Caribbean pursuit. Several cruise lines
offer sailing trips as a shore excursion
option.

Food and Drink

*C*aribbean cooking has few pretensions, but many influences. Aromatic pepperpot stews, Jamaican jerk (chicken or pork cooked over a barbecue pit), curried goat, and vegetable dishes, such as okra, callaloo soup (similar to spinach), fried plantains, and breadfruit are all West Indian staples with an African influence. In the French islands, there is marvelous Creole cooking, a fusion of French and African ideas; Trinidadians snack on *roti* (Indian-style unleavened bread filled with meat or vegetable); and Puerto Ricans enjoy *arroz con pollo*, a Caribbean-influenced rice and chicken dish cooked in coconut milk. There is plenty of fresh seafood, including lobster, shrimp, crab, flying fish (excellent in a sandwich), and conch (pronounced *conk,* and also known as lambi), a rubbery mollusc served up in fritters and stews from the Florida Keys to Trinidad. Fresh fruits, such as bananas, mangoes, pineapples, and guava ripened on the tree, taste twice as good as they do back home. Be sure to sample lesser known but perfectly delicious fruits such as golden apple (often served as a fruit juice) and superb soursop ice-creams. And no visit to Key West would be complete without a generous slice of Key Lime Pie.

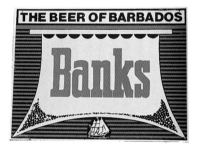

Tasty local beers are brewed throughout the Caribbean

DRINKS

There are dark rums, white rums, gold rums, and spiced rums. Some are so strong, like Trinidadian Jack Iron (160 percent proof), they can even sink ice. And the pirate Blackbeard is said to have spiked his rum with a sprinkle of gunpowder. Rum is the basic ingredient of cocktail hour in the Caribbean. It is used in Planter's Punch (add water, a twist of lime, and a sprinkle of nutmeg), piña coladas (add pineapple juice and coconut cream), and iced daiquiris (whizzed up with lime juice, crushed ice, and fruit syrup). Wine is imported and thus expensive in the West Indies, so most visitors stick to cocktails or sample the local beers, such as Red Stripe in Jamaica, Banks in Barbados, or the ubiquitous Carib from Trinidad.

The best nonalcoholic beverages feature local fruits, such as mango, golden apple, and fresh orange juice. Fruit punch is also very refreshing, and do try fresh coconut milk straight from the nut, or sweet sugarcane juice.

Spicy jerk pork is said to have been invented by runaway slaves in the hills

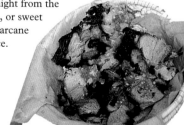

Jamaican ackee grows on trees and is served for breakfast with saltfish

WHERE TO EAT

This is a brief summary of restaurants and cafés throughout the region. The price brackets refer to a two-course meal without drinks:

$ – under $15 per person
$$ – between $15–20 per person
$$$ – over $20 per person

MIAMI
Astor Place Bar and Grill $$$
Elegant atrium setting for innovative Mediterranean/Pacific Rim cuisine.
956 Washington Avenue, Miami Beach. Tel: (305) 672 7217.
Joe's Stone Crab Restaurant $–$$
A local institution with "early Miami-Beach décor." Open October to May only.
227 Biscayne Street, South Miami Beach. Tel: (305) 673 0365. No reservations.
Victor's Café $$–$$$
Lively and attractive Old Havana-style restaurant serving great Cuban food.
2340 SW 32nd Avenue, Little Havana. Tel: (305) 445 1313.

FORT LAUDERDALE
15th Street Fisheries $$
Award-winning Florida seafood restaurant on the banks of the Intracoastal Waterway.
1900 SE 15th Street. Tel: (954) 763 2777.
Mark's Las Olas $$$
Sophisticated Florida fusion cuisine. Dinner reservations required.
1035 E Las Olas Boulevard. Tel: (954) 463 1000.
Riverwalk Brewery $
Good pit stop near the Riverwalk. Hearty sandwiches and salads, barbecues and home-brewed beers.

111 SW 2nd Avenue. Tel: (954) 764 8448.

KEY WEST
Louie's Backyard $$$
Innovative and delicious New World cuisine. Arty setting; chic clientele.
700 Waddell Avenue. Tel: (305) 294 1061.
Pepe's $–$$
Popular local diner with excellent food, barbecues, and leafy garden.
806 Caroline Street. Tel: (305) 294 7192.

Thirsty visitors to Key West can find a cure at Hemingway's original watering hole

Many old colonial homes have been transformed into atmospheric restaurants

ARUBA

Gasparito $$
Arty Aruban house serving local food. Shrimp en coco recommended.
Gasparito 3. Tel: (297) 8637044.

BAHAMAS

Pick A Dilly at the Parliament $$
Good island cooking, seafood, and pasta dishes. Notably good daiquiris.
18 Parliament Street, Nassau, New Providence. Tel: (242) 322 2836.

Pier One $$–$$$
Waterfront fish restaurant with fine harbor views.
Freeport Harbour, Freeport, Grand Bahama. Tel: (242) 352 6674.

BARBADOS

Atlantis Hotel $$–$$$
Excellent luncheon buffet, ocean views. Convenient for Andromeda Gardens.
Bathsheba, St. Joseph. Tel: (246) 433 9445.

Pisces $$
Caribbean seafood specialties served on the waterfront.
St. Lawrence Gap, Christ Church. Tel: (246) 435 6564.

ANTIGUA

Admiral's Inn $–$$
Light lunches with waterfront views from the garden terrace. Historic building.
Nelson's Dockyard, English Harbour. Tel: (268) 460 1027.

Hemingway's $
Huge sandwiches, flying-fish burgers, Key Lime Pie.
St. Mary's Street, St. John's. Tel: (268) 462 2763.

BERMUDA

Carriage House $$–$$$
International and local cuisine at the attractively restored wharf complex.
Somers Wharf, Water Street, St. George's. Tel: (441) 297 1270.

Frog & Onion $$
Good English-style pub grub served up in a restored dockyard building. Popular.

Romantic appeal: balmy evenings and alfresco dining by candlelight

*The Cooperage, Royal Naval Dockyard.
Tel: (441) 234 2900.*

CAYMAN ISLANDS
Cracked Conch By The Sea $$
Nautical décor, lively crowd, steaks, chowder, many variations on conch.
Rum Point, Grand Cayman. Tel: (345) 945 5217.

The Wharf $$$
Great seafood, continental and Caribbean dishes. Waterfront terrace with views.
West Bay Road, Seven Mile Beach, Grand Cayman. Tel: (345) 949 2231.

CURAÇAO
Bistro Le Clochard $$–$$$
Atmospheric dining in an 18th-century fortress jail. Swiss-French cuisine.
Rif Fort, Otrabanda, Willemstad. Tel: (599) 462 5666. Closed Sundays.

Cactus Club $
Popular local hamburger joint.
Van Staverenweg 6. Tel: (599) 737 1600.

DOMINICA
Papillote Wilderness Retreat $
Flying-fish sandwiches, omelettes, and salads on the shaded terrace.
Trafalgar Falls, Roseau. Tel: (767) 441 82287.

This typical Barbadian rum shop serves the "national drink," distilled from molasses

"Yo, ho, ho, and a bottle of rum" – the pirates' favorite tipple remains popular

GRENADA
Coconut Beach $$–$$$
French Creole waterfront beach restaurant. Lobster a specialty.
Grand Anse Beach. Tel: (473) 444 4644.

Morne Fendue $
Comfy, welcoming plantation house off the beaten track. Generous portions of local food (lunch only).
St. Patrick District, southeast of Sauters. Tel: (473) 440 9330.

GUADELOUPE
Le Karacoli $$
Great French-Creole food served on the terrace at Grande Anse beach.
Deshaies. Tel: (590) 28 41 17.

Au Mérou d'Or $$
Waterfront fish restaurant.
Gosier. Tel: (590) 84 02 27.

JAMAICA
Almond Tree $$–$$$
Lovely sea views and pretty surroundings. Jamaican-European food.
Hibiscus Lodge Hotel, 83 Main Street, Ocho Rios. Tel: (876) 974 2813.

Pork Pit $
Spicy Jamaican pork or chicken jerk cooked on a bed of coals.
27 Gloucester Avenue, Montego Bay. Tel: (876) 952 1046.

Four thousand miles from Paris, diners can enjoy gourmet French cuisine in Marigot

Anse de Grande Saline (1km). Tel: (590) 27 72 12.

ST. CROIX
Blue Moon $
Sidewalk tables and dining room in old Danish arcaded house. Good New World cuisine.
Waterfront, Frederiksted. Tel: (809) 772 2222.
Comanche $$
Casual atmosphere, terrace dining, and broad-ranging menu.
1 Strandgade, Christiansted. Tel: (809) 773 2665.

ST. KITT'S AND NEVIS
Ballahoo $
Salads, burgers, BBQ chicken wings, seafood platters; overlooking The Circus.
Basseterre, St. Kitts. Tel: (869) 465 4197.
Eddy's $
Hamburgers, BLTs, fruit punch, and ice-cream. Friendly spot.
Main Street, Charlestown, Nevis. Tel: (869) 469 5958.
(For other recommended restaurants on Nevis, see page 117.)

ST. LUCIA
Green Parrot $$
French and Creole menu, plus salads and grand views from the terrace.
Morne Fortune, Castries. Tel: (758) 452 3167.
The Lime $–$$
A friendly crowd and outdoor patio. Tasty fish fritters and sandwiches, burgers, and salads.
Rodney Bay. Tel: (758) 452 0761.

MARTINIQUE
Chez Gaston $–$$
Traditional bistro with French and Creole specialties.
Rue Félix Eboué, Fort-de-France. Tel: (596) 71 59 71.

PUERTO RICO
Chef Marisoll Cuisine $$
Contemporary Puerto Rican cuisine from one of the islands top chefs, Marisoll Hernández.
102 Calle Cristo, San Juan. Tel: (787) 725 7454.
El Patio de Sam $$
Patio-style dining, potted plants, and Latin-Caribbean influenced food.
Plaza de San Juan, San Juan. Tel: (787) 723 1149.

ST. BARTHÉLEMY
Le Tamarin $$–$$$
Delicious salads and fish a specialty.

Waterfront restaurants at Philipsburg on Dutch Sint Maarten

ST. MARTIN/SINT MAARTEN
Le Poisson d'Or $$$
Classic French cuisine in elegant surroundings. Terrace dining.
Rue de l'Anguille, Marigot. Tel:(590) 87 72 45 (first dial 00 from Dutch side).
Seafood Gallery $–$$
Popular pierside rawbar and seafood restaurant.
Bobby's Marina, Philipsburg. Tel: (599–5) 23253 (first dial 00 from French side).

ST. THOMAS
Gladys' Café $
Chowders, sandwiches, burgers, and local dishes served in courtyard. Recommended fruit punch.
Behind 17 Main Street, Charlotte Amalie. Tel: (340) 774 6604.
Hervé's $$$
Splendid views of the harbor from the terrace, with an tempting French-American-Caribbean menu.
Government Hill, Charlotte Amalie. Tel: (340) 777 9703.

ST. VINCENT AND THE GRENADINES
Frangipani $$
Daily changing menu; seafood specials and snacks. Delightful tree-shaded waterfront terrace; friendly and informal.
Port Elizabeth, Bequia. Tel: (784) 458 3255.
French Restaurant $$$
French and Caribbean dishes, excellent seafood, waterfront veranda.
Villa, St. Vincent. Tel: (784) 458 4972.

A shady courtyard setting for Gladys' Café in Charlotte Amalie, St. Thomas

TORTOLA
Pusser's Outpost $–$$
Full international menu restaurant upstairs; deli sandwiches, pizzas, and English pub grub below.
Road Town. Tel: (284) 494 2467.

TRINIDAD AND TOBAGO
Old Donkey Cart House $$$
Attractive garden setting in an old house. Local and European cuisine. German wines a specialty of the Viennese owner.
Bacolet Street, Scarborough, Tobago. Tel: (868) 639 3551.
Veni Mangé $
Appealing local lunchspot in colorful old house serving spicy and delicious Trinidadian specialties.
67a Ariapita Avenue, Port of Spain, Trinidad. Tel: (868) 624 4597.

Cruising and Cruise Ships

During 1997, more than five million people decided to take a cruising vacation, and the numbers are increasing every year. Gone are the days when the average cruise passenger was as old as the hills, and as rich as Croesus. Today's cruisers come from all walks of life and every age range. Their interests are diverse and their expectations high.

Cruise lines have risen to the challenge in style. In order to keep up with the passenger boom and the demand for higher standards and better facilities, they are introducing new cruise vessels at the staggering rate of about one every three weeks. Never before has the potential passenger been confronted with such a wide choice.

For first-time cruisers, there is help available. Travel agents affiliated with CLIA (Cruise Lines International Association) and PSARA (Passenger Shipping Association Retail Agents) have special knowledge of the cruise market. There are also cruise agents who deal exclusively in cruise vacations, and they are often a good source of both special deals and last-minute discounts.

TYPES OF CRUISES

There are two basic itineraries: loop cruises, which start and end at the same port; and one-way cruises. One-way cruises tend to visit more ports and spend less time at sea. However, a loop cruise from San Juan, Puerto Rico, can visit up to six destinations in a week.

Just as today's cruise passengers are a diverse crowd, so are the cruising options that await them. The traditional mainstream cruise ships pride themselves on catering to a broad assortment of customers. They promise excellent food, modern facilities, a wide range of general activities, and evening entertainment. Most incorporate some form of children's program, too, particularly during school holidays.

The Caribbean cruise ship *Horizon* steams off to meet its namesake

Themed cruises

If you are looking for something with more than mainstream appeal, consider a themed cruise. This is an increasingly popular sector of the cruise market. Themes cover a broad spectrum, from the gently educational or cultural, such as computers or wine-tasting, to murder-mystery outings and sporting cruises. Golf or tennis cruises offer instruction, as well as stops for a practice on dry land.

Family cruises

Kids love cruising, and most cruise lines love families. This is reflected in a range of special deals and child-orientated activity programs (see pages 166–7). Discounted rates for children sharing a cabin with two adults start at around 50 percent of the full fare and then drop. Some cruise lines even allow children under 12 to travel "free" (though air fares and port taxes still need to be paid).

How long?

As a rule, short cruises are more popular with the younger end of the market. Cruises lasting 10 days or more tend to charge a significantly higher rate per day, and the average age of the passengers rises accordingly.

Cruise-stay vacations

Cruise-stay vacations provide the best of both worlds, and some excellent deals. They are a good option for first-time cruisers, or for families who want to combine a cruise with a trip to Florida; for example, take a seven-day cruise out of Miami or Fort Lauderdale and several cruise companies (or travel specialists, such as Virgin Holidays) can arrange an impressively discounted rate for seven nights in a Florida hotel at the beginning or end of your trip. The main embarkation ports in the Caribbean are San Juan, Puerto Rico; Nassau, in the Bahamas; and St. Thomas, USVI.

Optional onboard activities run the gamut, from morning exercise routines to bingo (left)
A mid-ocean haircut or beauty treatment is no problem (right)

TYPES OF CRUISE SHIPS

Cruise ships can be roughly divided into four main categories: deluxe, luxury, premium, and standard. Somewhere between the top-of-the-line deluxe cruise vessels, with an atmosphere similar to that of an exclusive private yacht, and the monster party ships plying the Bahamas route, with a high

Stylish presentation and gourmet food are an important part of the cruise experience

proportion of passengers in their 20s and 30s, there is something to suit everyone.

Deluxe

Small and perfectly designed, the deluxe cruise ship is effectively a floating luxury hotel with a capacity of fifty to two hundred passengers. Its hallmarks are gourmet cuisine, exemplary service, and a high staff/passenger ratio.

Prime examples of this exclusive cruise class are Cunard's Sea *Goddess I* and *Sea Goddess II*.

Luxury

Luxury-class vessels attract a sophisticated and high-spending crowd. They provide elegantly appointed and large cabins, all of which will be sea facing and some of which will have private verandas. Standards of cuisine are extremely high, and guests dress up for dinner. Facilities vary with the size of the ship, but generally there are fewer organized onboard events.

The emphasis here is on informal relaxation. Notable in this category is the *Radisson Diamond*, the world's only full-sized catamaran cruiser, which boasts a retractable marina with jet skis, snorkeling gear, and a netted pool area between the ship's hulls.

Premium

The majority of mainstream cruise vessels fall into the premium class. They are owned by experienced cruise companies, maintained and run to a high standard, and offer an enjoyable cruising holiday with good food, good facilities, and a broad range of entertainment and activities. Guests will have the opportunity to dress up for a couple of formal nights. At the top end of this category, Celebrity Cruises' stylish and well-equiped *Meridian* and modern *Horizon* and *Zenith* ships have a reputation for outstanding food and service.

Standard

Standard cruise vessels are aimed at a more casual crowd. It is difficult to typecast them, as they cover a broad spectrum, from the huge, modern party ships to rather older vessels with fewer modern facilities. Two things you can be sure of in this class: cabin space is likely to be confined, and menus will be relatively limited.

Is big beautiful?

The size of a cruise ship is no indication of its place on the luxury scale, though it is safe to assume that the bigger the ship, the more varied the onboard facilities will probably be. Similar to a floating resort, larger cruise vessels (700 or more passenger capacity) can offer a greater choice of public rooms, dining alternatives, fully equipped showrooms, and more polished entertainment, as well as plenty of deck space for pools and sunbathing.

The mega-ships, such as Carnival Cruise Lines' *Fantasy* (2,634-passenger capacity), and Princess cruises' *Sun Princess* (1,950 passengers), are like dazzling, futuristic cities afloat. However, with such a large number of guests on board, they are bound to be somewhat impersonal.

Smaller cruise ships are more flexible in many ways. Most notably, their shallow draft allows them to call at ports that are inaccessible to big ships. Onboard facilities may be more limited, but what there is can be positively hedonistic. Cunard's *Sea Goddess* ships (116-passenger capacity) are some of the most luxurious ships afloat, awash with champagne and caviar, carpeted with Oriental rugs, and equipped with state-of-the-art water sports facilities, launched from a stern platform.

Once an expensive luxury, most cruise vessels now offer cabins with sea views

Sail-cruise vessels

For a cruise experience with a difference, there are several sail-cruise ships plying Caribbean waters. The most authentic sailing ships are the reproduction four-masted tall ships, *Star Flyer* and *Star Clipper*, each carrying around 170 passengers, and wind-driven for around 80 percent of the time. The contemporary "wind-assisted" Windstar vessels (around 150 passengers) and the French-built Club Med ships (around 380 passengers) have computer-controlled sails, which may disappoint true sailing types.

Elaborate buffets are a chance for the chef and her or his team to show off their skills

Hotels & Accommodations

*V*acationers planning to add a couple of weeks, or just a few days, ashore onto their cruise can choose from a wide range of accommodations, both in Florida and the Caribbean. Hotels, resorts, and apartments come in all sizes and prices ranges, and there are particularly good deals to be found during the summer off-season. High-season prices in the Caribbean start in mid-December and end in mid-April. During October and November, many Caribbean hotels are closed. Florida's hotels tend to be open year-round, but most offer heavily discounted summer-season rates.

Cruise-stay packages organized through a cruise line or tour operator will specify hotel options. Independent travelers can obtain accommodations lists from local tourist offices (and their overseas branches), or consult a knowledgeable travel agent. Remember to check out local government taxes (six percent in Florida), which can add considerably to the quoted room price.

APARTMENTS AND EFFICIENCIES

A practical option for families and groups, self-catering apartment or condominium (condo) rental is popular with independent travelers who require flexibility. A minimum stay of three to seven days is usual. Family-oriented apartment-hotels typically offer shops, a pool, play areas, sports facilities, and dining facilities.

On the budget front, many hotels and motels provide efficiencies – spacious rooms with basic kitchen facilities.

PLANTATION HOTELS

A Caribbean specialty, these lovely – and often very luxurious – hotels occupy restored plantation houses dating from the 17th to 19th centuries. There are usually some rooms in the main house, but others will be in the grounds in converted outbuildings. The atmosphere is quiet, and facilities are limited to a pool, maybe a tennis court, and board games in the library. Most plantation hotels are away from the beach.

The Fontainebleau Resort in Miami offers every facility and luxury

The Crystal Palace Hotel on Cable Beach, New Providence

RESORTS
All-inclusives
Increasingly popular in the Caribbean, all-inclusive resorts charge a single price to cover everything – all meals and snacks, drinks, transportation, sports and water sports facilities, activities, and entertainment, even laundry and beauty treatments. The obvious advantage is budget control. The downside is that, by its very nature, this type of resort discourages customers from venturing out. Guests therefore rarely meet locals and miss out on such basic holiday pleasures as dining in real West Indian restaurants and exploring other parts of the island.

Couples-only
This is a slight variation on the all-inclusive theme, led by the Sandals Resorts chain, which has outposts all over the Caribbean. Most have good facilities, a range of entertainments, and the ability to arrange anything, from horseback riding to a wedding (best man and maid of honor supplied on request). Couples must be 18 or over.

Family
Most resorts provide some form of organized children's activities, while a number specialize in family vacations, offering a full daily program of activities and events for adults, as well as children of all ages. Trained counselors, day-care and baby-sitting facilities, and special children's menus are all part of the service. Naturally, Florida is well-supplied with family-style resorts, and Jamaica is probably the leader in the Caribbean.

Sports and spas
Some of the best Caribbean sports facilities are owned and operated by resort hotels. Florida's sports and spa resorts offer unbeatable facilities for golf and tennis enthusiasts. Health and beauty-conscious types can enjoy saunas, whirlpools, massage, diet advice, and a wide range of beauty treatments.

Practical Guide

CONTENTS

American and Canadian visitors do not require passports to visit any Caribbean country, but must have proof of identity, such as a voter registration card or driver's license. Visas are seldom necessary for nationals of other countries visiting the Caribbean islands. Again, a valid passport will suffice.

Cruise passengers commencing or ending their cruise in a Caribbean country will be required to fill out an immigration form. These are handed out onboard aircraft or the cruise ship. Immigration rules are strictly enforced throughout the region, and the immigration authorities will need to see an onward ticket. The accommodations section of the immigration form must be completed or entry may be refused.

Ground transportation

Where possible, arrange airport transfers through the cruise company. Arrivals at Miami, Fort Lauderdale, and Puerto Rico's San Juan airports will find taxis readily available. Most Caribbean airports have tourist information desks that advise on ground transportation and taxi fares.

The journey from Miami airport to the Port of Miami is around 30 minutes; from Fort Lauderdale airport to Port Everglades is 10 minutes; from San Juan's Luis Muñoz Marin airport to the Old Town cruise piers is 45 minutes. At Miami and Fort Lauderdale airports, SuperShuttle minibuses offer a quick and inexpensive door-to-door alternative to taxis or limos.

ARRIVING

British visitors and other nationals from countries participating in the U.S. Visa Waiver program simply require a valid passport and completed waiver form (supplied) to enter the U.S. or the U.S. Virgin Islands.

CHILDREN

See pages 166–7.

CLIMATE

The Caribbean Sea and its semicircle of islands lie in the tropics, so year-round temperatures remain high, with little variation. Though temperatures can top 100°F (38°C), this is a rare occurence, and the heat is generally tempered by cooling trade winds. Daytime temperatures in the Caribbean average between 78 and 86°F (26–30°C); night-time temperatures are around 59 to 64°F (15–18°C).

The coolest and driest months are at the height of the December to April season. May/June and October/November are wet, though tropical showers (particularly in rain forest areas) can occur year-round. "Hurricanes hardly happen," but if and when they do, they usually choose September.

CONVERSION TABLES

See overleaf.

WEATHER CONVERSION CHART
25.4mm = 1 inch
°F = 1.8 × °C + 32

CRIME

Violent crime is rare on the smaller Caribbean islands, but on larger and busier islands, such as Jamaica, Trinidad, or St. Thomas, it is unwise to walk down unlit streets or along the beach after dark. Petty theft is a problem, so keep a close watch on valuables. Do not leave watches, wallets, and cameras unattended on the beach. Carry cash in a money belt or waist pack.

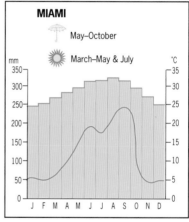

MIAMI
May–October
March–May & July

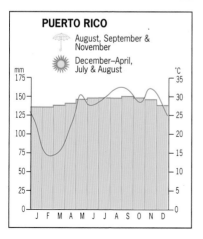

PUERTO RICO
August, September & November
December–April, July & August

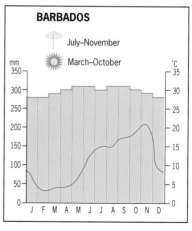

BARBADOS
July–November
March–October

Conversion Table

FROM	TO	MULTIPLY BY
Inches	Centimeters	2.54
Feet	Meters	0.3048
Yards	Meters	0.9144
Miles	Kilometeres	1.6090
Acres	Hectares	0.4047
Gallons	Liters	4.5460
Ounces	Grams	28.35
Pounds	Grams	453.6
Pounds	Kilograms	0.4536
Tons	Tonnes	1.0160

To convert back, for example from centimeters to inches, divide by the number in the third column.

Men's Suits

UK	36	38	40	42	44	46	48
Rest of Europe	46	48	50	52	54	56	58
US	36	38	40	42	44	46	48

Dress Sizes

UK		8	10	12	14	16	18
France		36	38	40	42	44	46
Italy		38	40	42	44	46	48
Rest of Europe		34	36	38	40	42	44
US		6	8	10	12	14	16

Men's Shirts

UK	14	14.5	15	15.5	16	16.5	17
Rest of Europe	36	37	38	39/40	41	42	43
US	14	14.5	15	15.5	16	16.5	17

Men's Shoes

UK	7	7.5	8.5	9.5	10.5	11
Rest of Europe	41	42	43	44	45	46
US	8	8.5	9.5	10.5	11.5	12

Women's Shoes

UK	4.5	5	5.5	6	6.5	7
Rest of Europe	38	38	39	39	40	41
US	6	6.5	7	7.5	8	8.5

Violent crime in Florida has been making the headlines for several years, though, to a large extent, the danger is limited to a handful of nontourist trouble spots, such as the Liberty City and Overtown districts of Miami. However, basic rules in any city advise you to leave any valuables in your hotel; carry only small amounts of cash; and always stick to busy, well-lit streets after dark. If in doubt, do not walk, but take a taxi instead.

Rental car companies in Florida hand out a list of simple safety precautions that should be observed. In the event of an accident, find a well-lit telephone – gas stations, stores, or restaurants are recommended – and dial 911. This call is free, even from pay phones, and connects with local emergency services.

CUSTOMS REGULATIONS

Alcohol and tobacco allowances vary from island to island. As a rule, the limit stands at around 1 liter of spirits and 200 cigarettes for every adult (over 18), as in the U.S. Visitors from the U.S. can re-enter the States with up to $400 worth of duty-free goods, or $1,200 if returning from the U.S. Virgin Islands. British visitors have an allowance of £136 on returning to the U.K. Foreign travelers departing from the U.S. within 48 hours are exempt from U.S. customs duties. It is important to remember that black coral and turtle products cannot be imported into the U.S., U.K., and many other countries.

DEPARTURE TAX

Most Caribbean islands levy a departure tax on visitors. Cruise passengers do not pay this unless they are flying home from one of the islands. The actual amount varies from island to island, though it is

around EC$25 (see **Money Matters**).
U.S. dollars are usually accepted.

DRIVING AND CAR RENTAL
Car rental is readily available on most
islands, but few cruise passengers with a
limited stay choose to take up the option.
In addition to a full national or
international driver's license, several
Caribbean islands also require drivers
to purchase a temporary local license
(usually available from the rental car
company), which adds to the cost. Check
the type of insurance the rental company
provides *very carefully*. Often the driver is
liable for the first U.S.$1,000 of any
damage done to the vehicle. Some
islands drive on the left, some on the
right, and some are swopping from one
system to the other, so nobody seems too
sure. Caribbean roads and drivers are
"adventurous." Perhaps too adventurous
for a relaxing day out.

Car rental in Florida is inexpensive
and easy. All the major car rental
agencies have concessions throughout
the state. Fly-drive deals can offer
excellent value for money and gas is
cheap. Driving is on the right. The top
speed limit on the highway is 55mph; on
some sections of interstate roads this is
raised to 65mph.

ELECTRICITY
The electrical current in the U.S. and
U.S. Virgin Islands is 110 volts AC.
Most other Caribbean islands have a 220
volt electricity supply. Cruise passengers
with electrical equipment, such as
shavers and hairdryers, should check
with the cruise line.

EMERGENCIES
In the U.S., the police and emergency
services can be summoned by a free call

to 911. In the Caribbean islands, the
numbers vary and may be anything from
three to seven digits long. Free brochures
from the local tourist office usually list
all the useful numbers on the island.
Pick one up before leaving the main
town.

ETIQUETTE
Dress is invariably casual in the
Caribbean and in Florida. Few
restaurants require men to wear a jacket,
and ties are almost extinct. Topless
bathing is forbidden in Florida and on
all but the French Caribbean islands.
However, it is unofficially sanctioned on
certain sections of many Caribbean
beaches.

HEALTH

No inoculations or vaccinations are required for visits to the Caribbean or Florida. Tap water is drinkable in most Caribbean countries, but buy bottled water and avoid drinks with ice on less-developed islands.

Do not let sunburn ruin your vacation. Be sure to use a high-factor sunscreen, and keep visits to the beach or pool deck short for the first few days. Mosquitoes can be a real problem for visitors to Florida's Everglades, and certain Caribbean islands in the summer season. Wise travelers carry a plentiful supply of repellent. Another potential health hazard is the machineel tree. Tall, bushy, and fond of a beachfront situation, the machineel has highly poisonous apple-like fruit and milky sap that can cause painful blisters and swelling if it comes into contact with skin. Do not even shelter under these trees in a downpour.

All cruise ships have a doctor, and some have infirmaries equipped to cope with emergencies. Passengers taking strong medication or with a condition that might require treatment during the cruise should inform the cruise line in advance and re-notify the ship's doctor soon after embarking.

MEDIA

Most cruise ships have satellite access to American cable news. American periodicals are sold around the Caribbean.

MONEY MATTERS

The U.S. dollar is local currency in Puerto Rico and the U.S. and British Virgin Islands. The common currency in the Eastern Caribbean is the Eastern Caribbean dollar (EC$), which has a fixed rate of exchange against the U.S.

dollar, as has the Bermuda dollar (BD$). The Bahamanian dollar is kept at par with the U.S.$; while the Jamaican dollar (JM$) and the Trinidad and Tobago dollar (TT$) fluctuate. French islands use the French franc; Dutch islands tender the guilder. U.S. dollars are widely accepted throughout the islands, but change will probably be given in local currency.

Credit cards and travelers' checks are used widely to free tourists from the hazards of carrying large amounts of cash. Although some countries accept other denominations, Thomas Cook recommends U.S. dollar checks. These can frequently be used to settle bills in larger restaurants, and tourist shops, without the need to cash them first.

TELEPHONES

The Caribbean telephone system is generally efficient and easy to use. There are plenty of public telephones that operate with coins and telephone cards. Cards are recommended for making direct-dial international calls. They can be bought from post offices, many shops, and information offices.

Making an international call from a public telephone in the U.S. is not so easy, as they only accept coins. The alternative to a manic coin juggling act is to dial the operator (0) and place a collect (reverse charge call) or telephone credit card call.

TIME

Eastern Florida, the Bahamas, and Jamaica observe Eastern Standard Time (GMT minus 5 hours). Bermuda and the rest of the Caribbean countries are an hour ahead (GMT minus 4 hours).

TIPPING

Tipping is one of the "hidden extras"

most cruise passengers have to face. Some luxury cruise ships have abolished it, some have an optional tips policy, but on most cruise vessels tips comprise an important slice of the staff's income. It is customary to tip the dining room staff and cabin steward on the last night on board. Most cruise lines provide tipping guidelines, and a list may be left in your cabin along with envelopes marked with the names recipients. As a basic guide, expect to tip the regular waiter and cabin steward U.S.$2.50 and the busperson U.S.$1.50 per passenger per day; the *maître d'hôtel* U.S.$5 for the whole trip; and the wine steward 15 percent of the wine bill. All tips should be in cash (preferably U.S. dollars). Bar stewards can be tipped during the cruise.

On land, tipping is expected in both Florida and the Caribbean. Taxi drivers expect ten to 15 percent; tip 15 to 20 percent for restaurant bills if service is not included. Tip bellhops U.S.$1/ EC$2.50 per item.

TOURIST INFORMATION

In many cruise ports, there is a tourist office or tourist information point located on the pier. They will be able to provide maps, taxi fare guidelines, and assistance with general inquiries about car rental, shopping, sports facilities, walking tours, and hiking guides. For vacationers who would like additional information or accommodations lists before departure, many Caribbean countries have overseas offices in the U.S. and U.K., as well as head offices that you will find listed throughout this guide.

TRAVELERS WITH DISABILITIES

Many cruise lines are wary of disabled travelers, and their attitude is far from encouraging. Others have modified cabins to provide a wheelchair-friendly layout. It is important to make detailed inquiries well in advance of the proposed travel date and supply as much information about special needs as possible. Contact a specialist cruise agency, such as Paul Mundy Cruising Ltd., Quadrant House, 80–82 Regent Street, London W1R 6JB (tel: (0171) 734 4404. In the U.S., Flying Wheels Travel, Box 382, 143 W Bridge Street, Owatonna, MN 55060 (tel: (507) 451 5005 or (800) 535 6790), is an agency which specializes in advising on cruise holidays for travelers with mobility problems.

ACKNOWLEDGEMENTS
The Automobile Association wishes to thank the following photographers and libraries for their assistance in the preparation of this book.
BERMUDA TOURISM 66, 67
SOPHIE CAMPBELL 70, 71
CELEBRITY CRUISES 16, 17
MARY EVANS PICTURE LIBRARY 82a, 82b, 82c, 83a, 83b, 102a, 102b, 103a, 103b, 103c
FOOTPRINTS 61 (A Misiewicz)
GREATER FORT LAUDERDALE CONVENTION & VISITORS BUREAU 36, 37a, 37b
JAMES HENDERSON 76, 117a, 117b
NATURE PHOTOGRAPHERS LTD 40a, 41c (J Hancock)
PICTURES COLOUR LIBRARY 1, 4, 25b, 52, 55, 56a, 56b, 57b, 79, 84, 92, 95, 98, 104, 105, 106, 107, 109, 111, 113, 128, 131, 147, 178, 180
REDFERNS 133b (D Redfern)
SPECTRUM COLOUR LIBRARY 34
ZEFA PICTURES LTD 19, 38, 40b, 136, 137, 164, 170
The remaining photographs are held in the Association's own photo library (AA PHOTO LIBRARY) and were taken by David Lyons, with the exception of pages 9, 10, 12, 13, 14, 48, 58, 59, 62a, 62b, 63, 74, 77, 78, 80, 81, 86, 87, 88, 89, 100, 101, 114, 121, 123, 124, 129, 130, 132a, 132b, 134, 135, 138, 139a, 139b, 140, 141a, 141b, 145, 146, 150a, 150b, 151, 152a, 153, 157a, 157b, 160a, 160b, 161a, 161b, 169b, 172a, 174a, 175a, 175b, 176, 177a, 177b and 187 taken by Peter Baker; page 18 taken by Jon Davison; pages 20, 24, 25a, 26b, 28, 29, 39a, 41b, 42, 154, 155, 168, and 184 taken by Pete Bennett; pages 23, 26a, 39b, 43, and 173b taken by Lanny Provo; pages 91, 93, 94, 96, 97a, 149a, 149b, 159a, 159b, 169a, 172b, 173a and 174b taken by Roy Victor; and pages 97b and 184 taken by Jon Wyand.
The author would like to thank the following people and companies for their help: Celebrity Cruises; Virgin Airways; Rosanna Albani, Condado Beach Hotel, San Juan, Puerto Rico; Montpellier Plantation Inn, Nevis; and the many helpful tourist office representatives who assisted the author.

CONTRIBUTORS
Series adviser: Melissa Shales   **Copy editor:** Paul Murphy   **Indexer:** Marie Lorimer
Thanks to **Emma Stanford** for her updating work on this revised edition.